AISLEY

AISLEYNE

Surviving Guns, Gangs and Glamour

Aisleyne Horgan-Wallace

MAINSTREAM
PUBLISHING

EDINBURGH AND LONDON

First published in Great Britain in 2009 by
MAINSTREAM PUBLISHING COMPANY
(EDINBURGH) LTD
7 Albany Street
Edinburgh EH1 3UG

ISBN 9781845964368

A catalogue record for this book is available
from the British Library

Typeset in Avant Garde Gothic and Sabon

Printed in Great Britain by
Clays Ltd, St Ives plc

ACKNOWLEDGEMENTS

Writing this book, editing this book and reliving this book has to be one of the hardest things I have ever done, but I am glad I did it. I have wanted to write my story down for years, way before I found myself in the spotlight. My book is a story about real life and trying to keep your head above water and showing the finger to 'statistics'.

I want to thank, and dedicate my book to, my parents. Thank you for falling in love, thank you for making me, thank you for loving me.

I want to thank anyone who has loved me, liked me or given me a chance in life. All my friends (too many to mention by name), my family (the ones who have stuck by me and the ones who have not) and my fans, who are a constant source of confidence to me.

If this book can inspire just one person to change their life for the good, then my desire has been accomplished and it will all have been worth it.

Thank you Bill Cambell for believing in my story; thank you Claire Rose for your patience and kindness through the editing stage. Thank you to Richard and to everyone who helped make this happen.

I believe everyone has the ability to defy the odds and achieve their dreams, regardless of what life may throw at you.

CONTENTS

INTRODUCTION

BLOOD ON THE FLOOR

I had to protect my dad. He was in trouble. He was in our bathroom crying out my name and all these policemen were trying to get at him. I tried to push past them all. I tried to get to the bathroom door to tell Dad I was there for him. But I got forced back. I got thrown back into my bedroom. I was four years old.

I'd been woken up by all the shouting. Maybe Mum had called the police; maybe it was some terrified neighbour. Whatever the reason, they turned up and stormed into our little flat in the middle of the night. I stood at my bedroom door and watched them through tears. Was this real or was it a nightmare? What was going on? I loved my dad so much. Why were all these men angry with him? The police all looked so big. For some reason, I remember they all had short hair. Their uniforms were harsh and black. When one of the policemen caught my eye, he looked as scared as me.

'Mummy, what's happening?'

I'll always be able to picture my mum standing right there in the middle of the hall she had only just finished decorating. She was crying too. 'Get back in your room,' she shouted at me. But I wouldn't. I couldn't.

'I just want to see my daughter,' Dad was shouting out from the bathroom. I tried to get through the policemen's legs again. This time, one of them grabbed me. I got pushed into my mum's room.

The man slammed the door behind me, only just missing my fingers. All I could do was listen to the madness on the other side.

'Police! Open the door!' Out in the hall they shouted it again and again, but nothing happened. Then it all seemed to go quiet. I came out of Mum's room and looked around. The police were still there. Mum was still there. Everyone was standing as still as statues, just looking at the line of light under the bathroom door. The door clicked open. The policeman in front of me moved forward. Suddenly, I had a perfect view of hell. I could see my dad's whole body, framed against the bright white tiles of our bathroom. He had his shirt off. He was covered in blood. He was holding a knife against one wrist while even more blood gushed out of the other.

'I just want to see my baby. I love you, Aisleyne,' he said.

'Put the knife down!' shouted the policeman right in front of him.

'Where's my princess?' Dad shouted as more blood hit the bathroom floor and splashed out into the hall.

I loved him so much. I didn't understand why he couldn't see me. I called out, waved and tried to push forward again. That was when the police jumped him. Dad disappeared underneath a pile of bodies. I started to scream, 'Don't hurt him, don't hurt him! Leave my dad alone!' Mum grabbed me. She pushed me back into her room again. She told me everything would be OK. She looked as scared as all the others. I sat on the crazy carpet of her bedroom and cried my eyes out. I knew I'd let my dad down. I hadn't been able to help him when he needed me the most.

The next thing I remember is how quiet the flat was when everyone had gone. Mum scooped me up and held me tight. She told me Dad had been very bad. 'But why was he crying?' I kept asking. 'Why couldn't I see him?'

I slept in my mum's bed that night. I loved that. Mum was so warm and I felt so safe there. The next day, we spent the whole morning in bed. Then we went out to the hall and the bathroom and I watched her clean everything up. Mum had loud music playing but it still felt like the quietest day of my life.

That night, I slept in Mum's arms again. 'Will they be looking after Daddy?' I asked as I drifted away to sleep.

'Of course they will. He's got lots of doctors and nurses looking after him now, and they're going to make him better,' she said. That made me happy. I never wanted him to be on his own.

● ● ●

Don't worry, it's not all like this. I've had my share of ups and downs. We all have. But what I have learned is that life is way too short to let negativity eat away at you. You have to learn from every situation and live life like you love it.

CHAPTER ONE

———————————————————●———————————————————

FASHION QUEEN

Dad was my mum's toy boy. They met at a squat party on the World's End Estate down the Kings Road in Chelsea. It was the late 1970s. Sophia Horgan was 19 and Steven Wallace had just turned 16. 'He was wearing skintight yellow cycling shorts and a cut-off black T-shirt that didn't reach his belly button. He looked a complete wally, a proper show-off,' she told me. But he was big and muscular with blond Billy Idol hair. She must have thought he was fit or I wouldn't be here now.

Mum had just finished at art college and she was what I would call a proper original, really unique. She was right at the heart of the punk scene. She went to every major party and gig in London. She knew everyone and everyone knew her. She had big dreams and lots of ambition right from the start. Her whole life revolved around fashion. She designed all her own clothes and dressed Siouxsie Sioux, Poly Styrene from X-Ray Spex and Boy George, as well as all her other friends. Safety pins, leather, plastic, zips and chains – her designs were full of punk spirit. She never stopped coming up with new ideas and her stuff was in demand 24/7.

Dad was interested in clothes too, but in a slightly different way. He and his mates used to race up to designer stores on their motorbikes, smash and grab whole racks of leather jackets, then speed off into the distance. Forget poetic justice, it was punk justice they were after back then. They said the shops were legally robbing off the public daily so they thought it was justified to turn the tables on them.

Looking back, it's a bit hard to see why Mum and Dad got on as well as they did. She was a hardcore punk and Dad was one of the last of the mods. When it came to music, clothes and mates they were quite different, but they were both rebels. They connected; they made it work. Dad's surname was Wallace and Mum was one of the very few people who got to call him 'Wally'. If the wrong person called him that, they were in trouble. I loved that Mum was able to use the nickname all the time. It proved they were equals.

Dad was always ready to help Mum perfect her new designs. My mum told me that one time she wanted to check out the detailing on some guy's leather jacket at a punk gig, so she told Dad to get it off him. Reluctantly (I would like to think), he nicked it for her – while the poor bloke was still wearing it. God knows how he managed it, but he did. Talented man, eh?

Mum thought it was hilarious. She and Dad just lived it large. No one on the scene had proper jobs. It was all art or music or fashion or drugs or something. Who the hell wanted to work in an office or a factory? And who could with bright green hair? It always sounded great when Mum told me stories about that time as I grew up. No wonder I never ended up with an office job myself.

My favourite story was the one about the day they got married. Well, sort of. Dad wanted to get married right from the start. He was old-fashioned like that. Mum was indifferent or maybe too independent. She didn't believe in marriage and she kept putting him off. Then, one night, he decided to just go for it. They were out together at the famous Tottenham pub at the end of Oxford Street. That was the place for everyone in the music and fashion worlds back then. It was my mum and dad's top haunt – they ruled it. That night, Dad left all their mates behind and dragged Mum out into the street. He got her across the road and dunked her in the fountain at the bottom of the Centre Point building. Then he carried her back into the Tottenham; it was sort of like carrying her across the threshold. Dad announced that they were now officially husband and wife, and all their mates went wild.

Dad reckoned that a quick 3 a.m. splash was as good as any church ceremony. As far as he was concerned, they were staying together. In the early hours, they went back to his flat for a joke honeymoon. The following afternoon, Dad got up, opened the curtains and turned on the radio. Forget punk – Bill Withers was on, singing 'Lovely Day'. Mum and Dad decided that this would be their song.

They had been dating for less than a year and Mum hadn't even turned 21 when she found out she was pregnant. It was just after Dad got sent for his first two-month stint in a young offenders' unit. She had to tell him the news by letter. She got a reply saying he would never go inside again once he became a father. He was totally passionate about being a dad. He wanted to do everything right and turn his life around. He believed that he would be able to do it. Mum believed it too. Maybe that's why the bad things hit her so hard when it all went wrong.

They lived together for the rest of Mum's pregnancy and began making plans, but their lives were still pretty carefree and wild. Dad had a massive motorbike and when Mum was eight months pregnant she went out on the back of it. I don't know how she managed to hold on to him, because I weighed 9 lb 8 oz when I was born and was well on my way to being a big, fat baby. Dad started racing some mate of his and they crashed into the back of a bus. Mum had let go of him, and she flew right over my dad's head and over a car before landing on her back in the gutter.

'Sophia, it's a miracle that your spine and your baby survived,' the doctors told her in the Royal Free Hospital up in Hampstead. Mum always thinks things happen for a reason and the fact that we were saved meant first that I was a very special baby and second that God was watching over us. In her mind, this proved a very important point. It proved she was a survivor and it meant that I would be too. 'Aisleyne, you could have been taken away from me before you were even born, but you weren't,' she told me time and time again when I was a little girl. 'You were lucky, a very special baby.'

I was born at the Royal Free on 28 December 1978, a few weeks after the crash. Dad wasn't at Mum's side for the birth. He was back in a young offenders' institution. But they did let him out to visit us on the day I arrived. It meant we had some pretty unusual baby photos. My favourite was the one Mum used to have in a frame at home. There we all were: Mum smiling proudly, me fast asleep, Dad in a pair of handcuffs. Then there was another one. Dad's holding me and there's some other guy standing right next to him. 'Who's that man, Mummy?' I asked years later. 'He was your dad's probation officer.' It all seemed perfectly normal. It took me years to realise that our house was anything but.

I've always loved my mum's spirit. Until it all went wrong, she wouldn't let anything stand in her way. Back then, nothing stopped her living life to the full. 'I was a size eight before I got pregnant with you, and the day I left hospital I squeezed myself back into my size-eight black leather trousers,' she always told me with a smile. She also wore a pair of PVC boots with three-inch heels. She slipped over on the ice on Pond Street and nearly dropped me.

Mum didn't have too many good examples of how a new mum is supposed to act. Plus it's not like there's some rule book with all the dos and don'ts that you're given with every birth: 'Here you are, Miss Horgan, a baby girl and a guidebook, all for you.' Instead, you're left to wing it, to do the best that you can and what you think is right, and Mum did.

She set out to be the best mother ever. She would give me everything, do anything for me. But first she had to choose a name. Dad went for Chantelle and they tried that out for my first few weeks. But Mum didn't like it. She thought it was common. My mum's side of the family is Irish and just before the final deadline for signing the official documents she told her friends, 'I want something traditional, something Irish.' She said she thought Aisling was too harsh and Ashley too masculine, but she liked that general idea. 'I like Ash,' she told everybody. So she just added a twist of her own and created the name Aisleyne. 'A unique name for a unique baby,' she would tell me. I love my name now, but when I was a kid whenever the register was read by a new teacher I would wriggle with embarrassment 'cause no one ever said it right. When you're a kid, you just want to be ordinary. For years, that was all I ever wanted.

Having me around seemed to release some massive creative urge in my mum, and she'd not exactly been a workshy girl till then. So it all went crazy with me in her life. If she had to stay up all night feeding me, then she might as well get some work done at the same time. She began designing even more out-there clothes and finding ever more out-there friends to wear them. We lived in loads of different flats in the first few years and wherever we were, our door was always open. Every punk, musician, dress designer and artist in London seemed to hang out with us. Mum had met this tall, big-nosed Irish guy called George O'Dowd at the Tottenham. They were absolute bezzy mates for ages – way before the rest of the world met Boy George. She told me he would put me on his knee and sing to me. He would change my nappies, do my hair and dress me up like a little punk doll. Then there was Siouxsie Sioux and Poly Styrene and all the other singers and musicians. Siouxsie and Poly both babysat for me sometimes and sang me punk versions of all the old lullabies. Johnny Rotten and some of the others in the Sex Pistols crew were in Mum's gang as well.

Far from freezing my mum out for having a baby, it seems that everyone competed for my attention. I was the only little girl on the scene and I was passed around at gigs pretty much before I could walk. I got tired backstage at the 100 Club once during a Discharge concert and just made myself a little nest out of some leather jackets. I reckon I slept well in the *Big Brother* house because I was brought up in noisy, crowded rooms. However mad the producers tried to make that house, it couldn't compete with the ones I lived in as a little girl, or indeed as a teenager.

The only person who wasn't always around was my dad. He'd wanted so much to be the perfect father. Mum said he managed it, at the start. The trouble is I was so tiny then that I don't remember those days. When it all went wrong, Mum threw all our family photos away, so I don't have anything to prove that we were ever happy together. By the time I was three or four and could pay attention, I noticed that it was just me and Mum. Maybe that shouldn't have mattered. We had settled in a fourth-floor flat in Kentish Town and no one we knew really lived in a traditional world of mums, dads and 2.4 kids. But however happy I was with my mum, I used to dream of seeing my dad as well.

I had this endless craving for what I thought of as a normal, average life. A little while after we moved in to our flat, I jumped across from our balcony to our neighbours' balcony and back. They'd just put some shiny new pegs out on their washing line and I nicked some for Mum. She was furious. She marched me right round and made me apologise. I remember two things about that visit. One was that the old couple were just lovely. They were more worried that I could have killed myself leaping across to their balcony than they were about the pegs. I'd like to have seen more of them. The other was that their flat was so ordinary that I didn't want to leave.

It was the same on the few visits we made to my nan and grandad, my dad's parents. They had a shaggy Afghan dog called Toomac. My grandad practised his putting in the corridor. In the living room, they had a big display case all along one wall that contained everything, even their telly. It made it all so neat and lovely. I watched *The Wizard of Oz* there nearly every time I visited. It was all very safe and ordinary there, and I loved it. I was a neat freak as a little girl. I remember one time I threw up after drinking a bright-pink strawberry milkshake. I was mortified about making a mess in such a tidy kitchen.

Back with Mum, life was anything but tidy. Not that I'm saying that's a bad thing; it was exciting too. Our flat was where Mum worked as well as where we lived. We were surrounded by whole reams of fabric, books of swatches, piles of samples and all my mum's incredible sugar-paper patterns. What little girl wouldn't want to grow up surrounded by all that? Mum's figure drawing was incredible. To this day, I've never seen anyone match it for detail or flair. I grew up tracing her designs. I sat and watched, and learned how to create some crazy dress the same way I learned how to read and write. Fashion's in my blood and that's why I love designing my own clothes today.

Going out on the fashion trail with Mum taught me a lot too. That was always fun. Camden Market was Mum's favourite hunting ground. We'd spend day after day wandering round there with one or another of her designer friends. One was called Jan, a glam girl with bleached blonde hair; then there was a guy called Pete, who had big glasses and a ridiculously bad toupee. It looked home-made. He'd created a floor-length fake-fur coat for Boy George and he made me one just like it. Mine was white with bright-red polka dots, and the other kids at nursery school laughed at it. I dunno – no vision, these infants. Mum would examine everything on every stall in Camden. She had an amazing eye. In a rack of ordinary high-street knock-offs, she could spot the one item with flair. I'd watch her register what made that piece work. Then I'd wait at home to see how she would use those special elements in her own drawings, before being dragged over to Brick Lane or back to Camden to get the material to turn her pictures into reality.

In Brick Lane, it was only ever men who ran the fabric shops. They always seemed a bit suspicious of my punk mum and me, her little waif-and-stray wild child. In Camden, it was easier. Mum got most of her stuff from a tiny, dry stick of a woman, who couldn't care less what her customers dressed like. I thought the woman was a witch, partly because of the way she looked and partly because of the way she could lift huge rolls of material on her own. She had more strength than a weightlifter. She'd need it; Mum's clothes were getting noticed and she was about to begin making more of them than ever. She was going to make her dreams come true. Mum was opening her own shop.

My mum had done it all the hard way. For so long, she had been handing out clothes for free to get a buzz going. Finally, the influential style magazine *The Face* had printed loads of pictures of Siouxsie and Poly wearing them. They did a big interview with Mum as the hot new designer of the moment. They said she was inspirational and ahead of her time. I could have told them that and I was only a little girl. The article did the trick. Readers rang in to find out where they could buy her stuff, so Mum landed herself a shop – not a stall, a whole shop – in the old Kenny Market in west London. Kensington Market was the Carnaby Street or Kings Road of its day. Mum reckoned it was way cooler than Camden. It was the absolute best place to be for up-and-coming fashion designers. You couldn't just walk in and get a place like that without being good. Just as the magazine had said, my mum was the best. She was also a grafter. Sure, music still blared out of our flat and all the crazy friends still piled around every night, but through it all Mum kept on working. She kept her focus. In the run-up to the opening, I'd always be getting up in the morning to find

Mum still sitting with her designs, having worked all night. I could see how tired she was. But she was a perfectionist and I also knew how determined she was to get her designs just right.

Mum's shop was called Phrantik Psycho. It was deep inside the old market buildings on Kensington High Street. Now, I think of it as a kind of successor to Vivienne Westwood's Sex down at World's End. It was a perfect punk boutique. I loved everything about it. The market was a treasure trove of hidden corners and secret places to make dens. I grew up playing hide-and-seek there and got to know loads of the stallholders and shopkeepers. I played in the converted stables out the back as well as in all the shops and the stall areas inside. I made myself little dens in dark corners and tried on loads of stuff in the other shops. I rarely got scared but one place that always frightened me was the 'dungeon'. A thick, black velvet curtain covered the stairway and only special customers got to go through there. Downstairs were tailors' dummies dressed in the most extreme rubber, leather, fetish and S&M gear. Some of them had fake blood on their faces. The clothes racks were full of the most frightening stuff. I got freaked out every time I went down there.

Sometimes, though, I wasn't sure what scared me more: the dummies in the dungeon room or the customers who swarmed around the rest of the market. Mum had toned down some of her more out-there designs for the main shop, but Kensington Market still seemed to attract every punk in London – and the more extreme the better. Their hair, the piercings on their ears, lips, eyebrows and everywhere else were proper mental. But it was the safety pins and razor blades that worried me the most. I just could not figure out why my mum's friends put blades in their hair or round their necks. I was a little girl who had dreams about being as pretty as a princess. I liked pink things and long floaty dresses; I liked sparkling bracelets and necklaces with jewels. Mum hated walking through Marks & Spencer as a short cut from the Tube station to the shop, 'cause I would always run off and hide amongst the pretty girlie dresses that she said were mundane and boring. I remember one bloke who had tattoos all over his face, even on his eyelids. Every time he blinked, I was rigid with fear. Mum thought he was fabulous. Whenever she wanted to wind me up, she told me she was going out for a night and that this wild man was going to be my babysitter. I was always pretty sure it was a joke, but until George, Poly or one of the others came round I could never quite relax.

Living with such an artistic mum meant that the drawing and painting I did at nursery school was just an added bonus. We did enough of that at home. Mum and I were always playing, painting or changing our rooms around. I get some of the flats we stayed in during the early days mixed up when I look back today. But I remember the best bits of all of them. Our Kentish Town flat, where we stayed the longest, was magical. Mum painted a huge black and silver spider's web across all the walls in the hall. It went right down to the floor and right around all the corners. She turned my bedroom into a wonderland. I had pink furry wallpaper at one point, with a jet-black ceiling covered in ice-blue stars. Our kitchen stayed the same in almost every flat – bright yellow and really friendly – but the decor in the other rooms was always changing. During one phase, Mum's room had green and purple walls, an ink-black carpet, shiny white wardrobes and huge fake-fur curtains. One time, she kitted out the living room as a cross between a bar and a brothel. She'd found some wine-red pub wallpaper with thick velvet stripes, and we had two skulls by the fireplace – I guess that stopped 'em from catching cold! Mum's ideas always worked, even if written down it sounds as if it would clash. Our actual furniture was just as unique. Mum found great stuff on markets or in skips. She had an incredible eye. She could see potential in things that would look like just old junk to others.

I think I was a miniature adult even before I was old enough for primary school. You grow up fast when you're always hanging out with your mum at work. I liked grown-ups almost more than I liked kids my own age. I liked the attention they gave me. I liked being funny and making them laugh. I also liked stuffing my chubby little fist into their beers while they weren't looking and licking my hand clean after – yum! I was precocious. I noticed things, remembered things, stored up questions in my mind.

But I had a secret from my mum. I just kept on thinking about my dad. I used to look at his picture all the time at home. It was a tiny picture of him standing on a wall with his hair shaved short, wearing drainpipe jeans and a button-down shirt – typical mod gear. I wished I could magic him up out of thin air. I wanted to ask him questions, to have days out with him, to feel that he was looking after me and would make my life safe. So where was he? Somehow, I knew I wasn't supposed to ask. I heard my mum and her friends talk about prison sometimes and rehab at other times, and I sort of knew Dad must be somewhere like that. But I knew people didn't stay in those places for ever. I just kept on hoping that one day Dad would turn up and we would be a real family, like the ones on TV. I prayed for this at night. I woke up every morning hoping he might have turned up while I was sleeping. Funny that he ended up doing just that – and that it didn't exactly have a happy ending.

CHAPTER TWO

●

DAD'S BACK

He climbed in through our bathroom window. It was a small window and he was a big man. We were on the fourth floor.

'Shush, princess, shush. Daddy's come back to see ya. He doesn't want to wake up your mummy.' Dad had crept into my bedroom and woken me up. I had never been as happy to see anyone in my short life. Didn't this prove that prayers really did get answered? Waking up to find his cold hand over my mouth and his worried eyes looking down at me didn't scare me at all. It was the best surprise ever.

'Are you gonna be quiet, baby?' I looked into those wide blue eyes and tried to nod my head. I would have done anything to keep Dad there. When he took his hand off my mouth, I pulled myself up and threw myself at him. I wrapped my arms around him. He felt hot, really hot, and I kissed his hair, kissed his rough, stubbly cheek and started to cry.

'Remember, you've gotta be quiet, princess.' I tried so hard to do what he said. I just wanted to see a flash of his big white smile. I wanted him to know how happy I was to see him. But I couldn't keep it inside. I was so cross with myself for crying that I started to sob even more. When my crying got too loud, Dad's hand went back on my mouth. So I toughened up. I nodded again to try and let him know I was OK. I watched as he stood up. Like I said, Dad's a big man, and I had a small room. He filled almost the whole space. I watched him walk around, looking at things, picking things up and putting them down, smiling at my teddies, wiping tears from his eyes when he looked at a photo of me and Mum, happy, smiling, together, without him. That killed me, and a piece of Dad must have died too, I think.

'I just wanted to see ya, baby,' he said when he'd composed himself. 'Go back to sleep.' He didn't lean over and hug me again. He looked like he was shaking all of a sudden, and he just sort of blew me a kiss, put his finger to his lips and went back into the hall. I was fizzing with excitement. I listened at my door. I don't know how I knew, but I felt sure Mum would be angry when she saw him. That was why she was always so careful about locking the door and why he'd had to break in just to see me. I was desperately hoping she would be happy and forgive him, even though I was too young to know what for. I started to pray that she would want him to come back and live with us again. I wanted Daddy to feel loved by us. I wanted that picture to be taken again, this time with Daddy in it too.

But five, maybe ten minutes later, it all went wrong. I could hear shouting through the bedroom door. On and on it went, round and round. 'Why are you here? How did you get in? What do you want?' Mum asked question after question. Dad just kept on saying the same thing: 'I just wanna see my princess.'

Mum shouted straight back at him, 'That's a lie. Who are you hiding from? What have you done?'

'No one. I ain't done nothing. I just wanna see you and my baby. Can't I stay with you?'

I wanted my mum to say yes more than anything. But she was angrier than I had ever heard her. Again and again, she asked what he was doing here. He said he had a present for me, and for some reason that made her even angrier. It sounded like they were running around or fighting. I heard her bedroom door bang open and their voices were even louder.

'Get out of here! Get out!' Mum screamed.

'All right! I'm leaving now and you will never see me again,' he yelled back. He didn't sound like my dad at all. I heard him kick over Mum's funky hall table. Then the chains on the front door were being pulled back and the locks were clicking. Dad had gone.

He'd come back into and out of my life so fast. Now all I could hear was my mum crying, for what felt like for ever. When she stopped, she came into my room. I don't think she knew Dad had been in to see me. I decided I'd keep that a secret. It made me feel better. I liked having a secret. 'Aisleyne, everything's going to be OK,' she said. She kissed my hair and hugged me. She was all shaky and she felt cold. 'You don't ever need to be scared again,' she said. That was the thing I didn't get. Why did she think I would be scared of my dad? He was my hero. He was the one I dreamed about every single night. He would never do anything to hurt me.

Before Mum went back to her room, I could hear her checking the locks on the door again. Then I heard her go into the bathroom. The next morning, I saw that she had tied the window shut with shoelaces. When I saw them, I realised exactly how Dad had got in and I was even more proud of him. He must have looked like Spiderman when he jumped from the hallway outside the flats to the balcony and then to the ledge outside the bathroom. He must have wanted to see me more than anything. I knew he was going to come back. A few bits of string wouldn't stop him.

The next night he broke in was the night he slit his wrists and got carried out by the police. I didn't see him again for more than a year. Mum never spoke about him once during that time. I didn't know if he was alive or dead and I was too scared to ask. All I could do was think about him and pray for him. Once, I tried to write him a little letter, though I was so young I think all I could manage was: 'I love you, Daddy.' My next attempt was more ambitious. I wrote a letter to God. I wanted to ask if God would look after my dad and make him well again. I wanted to ask if God would bring him back to live with me and Mum one day soon. I didn't manage to write much more than the last time, but a picture is worth a thousand words, right? So I covered the piece of paper in all my favourite stickers and put loads of glitter on it so God would know how important it was. I just wished I knew how to post it.

Meanwhile Mum was throwing herself into her work. She slogged her guts out and never stopped taking on new challenges. Making the clothes and running the shop took all her energy, yet she kept finding more. She had this idea for a new full-colour punk magazine. When her other work was done, she stayed up night after night writing articles for it, sorting out the photographs, then working out how to get it printed and sent to the shops. To be honest, I don't think it lasted for more than one or two issues, but Mum did get it published. How many other people achieve something like that?

Every part of her life in those days still inspires me now. She was tough as hell and always had a smart answer or a joke for everyone. Nothing scared her. No one could beat her. When I started at nursery school, one of the other parents jeered at her in the street for wearing one of her own-design fake-fur coats. 'Ignore her, Ash. She can laugh all she likes but everyone will be wearing coats like this in a year or two,' Mum told me as we strutted away, heads held high. She was right. She always was. That's why years later I found it hard to accept when the reality hit that we had different opinions on things. Learning that my amazing mum might possibly be wrong about stuff hit me so hard, I guess 'cause she was my be-all and end-all, my universe! I suppose that's how it is for a lot of kids raised by a single parent.

Mum wasn't the only one who got comments on her clothes. Forget Baby Gap, I was in crazy stuff from the start. Mum made me some amazing outfits and everything she got me to wear had people staring in the street. I wore electric bright colours – normally ones that clashed wildly. I remember one picture of me in a babygro with big fabric spikes down the outside of the sleeves and legs; one side was white, one black. I wore bright-yellow leggings, pink polka-dot coats, shiny plastic skirts with oversized white stitching on the seams. I looked like a bee one day, a Christmas tree the next. I can look back and appreciate it all now, but as a kid I thought it was torture!

'All the other girls'll be wearing them soon. It'll be just like my fur coat,' Mum said when she decided that big, baggy harem-style trousers would be the next big thing for tiny girls. She was right, yet again, but I had a lot of mortifying moments feeling like a clown before any of the other north London mums caught on.

When I was little, her fake-fur coat kept on getting her into trouble. One barney took place in a supermarket on Kentish Town Road.

'You're a killer. A murderer,' shouted an animal-rights enthusiast who hadn't looked at the fabric closely enough.

'Yes, I am. I'll have you know that I had to kill 104 teddy bears to make this coat,' Mum shouted back at him as we laughed our way to the checkout.

Then there was my big day out with Mum and my nan, Dad's mum. Mum was still at the height of her punk phase, and she dressed Nan up in black bin-liners and safety pins. She even gelled clumps of her hair into spikes and sprayed them different colours! Then we all headed off to the West End on the bus, where the conductor turned out to be the son of one of Nan's neighbours. Mum thought it was the funniest thing in the world. I did too, and so did Nan – in the end.

We didn't always see so much of my mum's side of the family. She had four brothers and two sisters, and at one point my auntie Ingrid moved to a new place and cut herself off for a while. We weren't having that, so Mum and I joined all the brothers, and we went off to talk to her. Her place was a nice, neat little house out on the edge of the city, with a big glass panel halfway down the front door. I was standing right in front of that panel when Uncle Dennis rang the bell. I could see Auntie Ingrid at the top of the stairs. She had obviously just got out of the shower. She was wrapped up in a towel and holding a toothbrush in her hand. 'How come you're so early?' she called out as she came down the stairs. She had a big, beaming smile on her face and I couldn't wait for her to look up and see us. When she did, she stopped suddenly and her smile disappeared. I'd never seen anyone's face change so completely or so fast. 'Oh, it's you,' she said. It was obvious she'd been expecting her boyfriend. While she didn't exactly slam the door in our faces, it took a while till she let us back into her new life – years, in fact. But even back then I understood why she needed a break.

Dad exploded back into our lives when I was about six. This time, he came in through the front door, not the bathroom window, but his return was almost as dramatic all the same. If Mum was a whirlwind, then Dad was a hurricane. Maybe that's why they found each other so exciting – and why there was always trouble when they were together. The madness began the moment Dad arrived.

He was such a big man, really well-muscled and over six feet tall. He still wore wild, bright colours. He was so big and so loud that he filled the flat with his presence. It was like having a giant move into our home. He was the most exciting person I had ever known. Always up, always on like a real-life Duracell bunny, he'd grab me and take me out of the flat, out on super-fast walks around the streets and to the park. He raced around the shops with me and bought me a sunflower, the most beautiful flower I'd ever seen. And there were the questions. He wanted to know who my friends were, he wanted to see my school, know where I went playing, hear whether or not I could read out loud – it just went on and on.

Or at least for a while it did. At some point, in the first few days when he and Mum were trying to make a go of it again, he just stopped. He'd curl up on Mum's bed or on the sofa in the living room and sleep. We tiptoed around him, but we didn't need to. When Dad slept nothing could wake him. I would sit on the floor next to him, just watching that huge chest rise and fall, listening to those incredible snores.

'Sophia, open the door!' Mum's friends were the ones who normally woke Dad up. This was their open house and they weren't used to our door being locked. With Dad awake and on his feet, Mum would decide she might as well let them in. That was when the fun began. Dad never really got on with Mum's punk friends. Right back when I'd been a baby, he'd been freaked out to find out that Boy George had a massive crush on him. The last thing Dad wanted was to be drooled over by some big Irish bloke wearing make-up and what he reckoned was a dress, so he made everyone's life hell for a while. George and his mates stopped coming around till Dad disappeared again. Now, five years later, history sort of repeated itself. I'd got used to saying goodnight to all the weird and wonderful characters in our lounge as I headed off to my room. I always knew that either the punks or the Goths or the fashion crowd or the musicians would still be there when I woke up the next morning. But after Dad came back, he began to head out when the day's first set of visitors arrived. Then he would come home late. I would stand behind my bedroom door listening as he forced them all to leave. 'You've got me now.

You don't need these freaks,' he'd shout at my mum when she tried to stop him.

One time, he grabbed a whole load of my mum's designs and threatened to throw them out of our window. 'You don't need to sell that stuff. I'll look after you now,' he told her as she tried to protect her work. Years later, I did *Romeo and Juliet* at school and I recognised my mum and dad as star-crossed lovers. They were two people who loved each other, were born to be together – but who couldn't live together. Now I know that however hard you try, love isn't enough for some people. It wasn't enough for us.

What made me happiest as a little girl? The times I heard my dad tell Mum that he loved her. 'I love you, I love you, I love you, I love you.' I was in my room in the middle of the night and Dad was shouting the words really loud. They didn't sound so nice that way. He was screaming and then after a while he was crying. Then he started yelling out those three words 'I love you' again and again. They really didn't sound nice any more. But for some reason I blamed my mum for Dad's mood swings. I asked her why she never told Dad that she loved him too. I said she had made him cry. I might even have told her that I hated her. If I did, I'm sorry. I wish I'd known more. I wish I hadn't been so young.

Looking back, I wonder whether Dad's changing energy levels and behaviour might have been signs that he was already struggling with drugs. I don't know. One thing I'm sure of, though, is that if someone around you suffers from severe mood swings, there may well be a reason, like drug use or health problems, behind it. The reason's not you and it's not your fault.

Mum just carried on. She always tried to calm Dad down. When he was asleep or out of the flat, she worked harder than ever. She made her own money and used it to give me all the things she thought I needed – toys, a new yellow bike tied up with a bright-red ribbon, all sorts of new clothes. We spent a lot more time at Phrantik Psycho while Dad was back. Then we started making new friends. I was well used to all the odd characters that made up Mum's world, but this latest crowd was different. They weren't punks or artists or musicians or Goths. They were Jehovah's Witnesses. All my life,

Mum had been holding some kind of audition to find a religion that could answer all her questions about life. The Witnesses were just the latest in a long line. She thought they could save her. She wanted them to save Dad as well.

CHAPTER THREE

FINDING RELIGION

When I was a baby, our local priest in Kentish Town had refused to christen me.

'I won't do it because you don't come to church and you've got green hair,' he told my mum.

'So does that mean that if my baby dies tomorrow she'll go straight to hell?' she asked.

'Yes, I'm afraid it does.'

The reply sort of put Mum off that particular church. But it didn't stop her looking for alternatives. When she shaved her head after becoming a Hare Krishna, I cried so much I thought I might die. I was about four or five and hadn't really noticed how odd that set of her friends looked. I think I actually preferred the Krishnas and their soft, colourful robes to the punks with their chains and zips and safety pins.

'Ash, you help everyone make some nice sandwiches and Mummy will be back in a while,' she said to me one day, before shutting the kitchen door and heading into the bathroom with some of the Krishnas.

'It's me, baby. What do you think?' she'd said when she walked back into the kitchen, dressed in her own set of robes, bald as a snooker ball and with the smoothest, palest and shiniest head I'd ever seen. What did I think? I thought I'd lost her. I didn't think I had a mum any more. I thought she was something from outer space.

But I got used to it, the way kids get used to everything. And to be honest, the whole Hare Krishna thing was pretty good for a while. The food at our temple was great. I'd be sent upstairs during the services or meetings, and there was always plenty to eat and drink. Trying on the robes was a bit of a laugh as well. They weren't quite the princess dresses I dreamed of wearing, but they were a bit nicer than all the rubber and leather stuff my mum made at home. So I enjoyed the temple visits. I even enjoyed the time I was bowing, like everyone else, to the goddess figure with her eight arms and I saw the statue wink at me. To this day, I swear it did. I saw it so clearly. Though maybe someone had just put acid in the lassi.

I could certainly understand it if the adults felt they needed something to give them the confidence to head out onto the street for the chanting processions through central London. Even then, I knew they were being laughed at, or worse.

The only thing I didn't like about the weekly Hare Krishna services was going to the loo. For reasons I never quite understood, they didn't have toilet paper. 'Just use this, Ash,' my mum said to me in the Ladies. I opened the cubicle door and she handed me a little china bowl of water. I was appalled. It was the first and last time I had a pee at the temple.

Being a Hare Krishna is all about peace and love and sweetness and light, right? Well, it was until my mum got really serious about it. Sure, she had embraced all the early-stage teachings and done the whole shaved head thing (even though that was actually meant to be something for the men, not the women – trust my mum to break down barriers and do it anyway). She had soaked up all the writings and the messages. But then she started asking questions.

Looking back, it makes no sense that on the nights when our flat was full of the punks and fashionistas it was calm, relaxed and – apart from the music – pretty quiet. Things only got heated on the nights when the Krishnas came round. That was when Mum fired questions at them. When, what, how and why, why, why? She always needed to know more than they seemed able to tell her. She had such an inquisitive mind and such incredible focus. She was like a dog with a bone. She got angry and simply would not let go of any argument. If the Krishnas told her a theory, she would pull it apart. If they read out one set of scriptures, she wanted to hear ten more. I admire my mother's passion and intensity. It wasn't that she was deliberately aggressive about it, even though she got amazingly heated when the others couldn't answer her questions. She just needed to be sure before she could truly believe. To get that security she had to see things from every angle. She had to ask every question and check that each argument was watertight. I'd go to sleep sometimes while the arguments went on. I'd wake up sometimes to find the Krishnas had all gone and Mum was just pacing around the flat, reading the texts and asking herself the same questions she had been asking them. She was trying to decide if she was ready to let go and really believe.

We went on a retreat somewhere while this phase was going on. I can still see my mum in this farmhouse, totally engrossed in conversation with all the others. As usual, I was bored, so I headed off down the lane, without telling anyone, to try and have an adventure of my own. This nutty woman came up to me. She wasn't speaking English – I can't quite remember, but I think we might have been abroad. Even if I'd been able to speak her language, though, I don't think she'd have made much sense. She grabbed me by my arm, dragged me into a nearby suburb and bundled me into her building. We went up in the lift and into her flat. Then the woman tried to put a nappy on me. I was four or five. It was bizarre. As I tried to stop her pulling my pants down, another little girl came into the room. She was just a bit older than me. I guessed that the mad woman was her mum. Again, I couldn't understand the language, but I could tell the other girl was pleading for me to be left alone. When the woman left the room, in floods of tears, the girl took me back outside. I ran all the way back to the farmhouse. My mum was still there, arguing the toss with the Krishnas. I was so freaked out by it that I didn't even tell anyone what had happened.

Mum stuck things out with the Krishnas for a while after that trip. I'm sure the people in the congregation had thought it was a huge coup to convert this wild, crazy punk woman to their faith. But I think they were already starting to regret it. After another six months or so, she was becoming too much for them and she could hardly sell the message to others when she had so many doubts herself. So we stopped going to the temple. Mum's hair grew back and she started to dye it rainbow colours again. The orange robes got recycled into some out-there new designs for Phrantik Psycho.

But Mum certainly wasn't finished with religion. She just needed to find the right one. We had a Buddhist phase, I believe. Then, I think, we became Hindus for about six months. I was pretty much the only white girl trying to make friends among all the Indian families way over in Wembley. We went to a lot of different temples around there and this time none of the statues winked at me. It was all OK while it lasted. I hardly remember anything of the lessons we learned, but the things I've picked up since tell me good things about the Hindu message. Some of Mum's punk friends actually ended up following her into that faith and found peace there. Mum mixed up two totally different worlds and made them work together. But it wasn't working for her. She never quite made it. Her questions kept on coming. So I left the Wembley girls without getting a chance to say goodbye and waited to see what Mum would stumble across next.

• • •

'You're not like all the others, Aisleyne. You're special. Didn't I always tell you that?'

'But Mum –'

'But nothing. You could have been taken away from me before you were even born, but you weren't. You're here for a reason. I won't let anything happen to you. I won't let anyone ruin your life.'

We were in my bedroom and we hadn't had any visitors for days. It was just after Dad had come back. Yet again, he had pretty much scared all Mum's punk friends away. She had just driven out her latest religious crowd. All I'd ever wanted was to live an ordinary life with my mum and dad. Now that I was doing it, things didn't seem as wonderful as I'd hoped. I felt I had to walk on eggshells all the time. The flat was quiet, empty and felt cold. If this was happy families, I'd got it all wrong.

'We don't need anyone else, Ash. We're fine just the way we are,' Mum said. I couldn't understand her. We needed Dad, didn't we? I asked if he was going to stay with us this time and she said she didn't know. She said he wasn't well. I pulled myself up from my bed. That was what she'd said after the night he'd cut his wrists. I started to cry because I didn't want him to do that again. 'He's going to be fine,' Mum told me. She was holding my hands but she wasn't really looking at me. 'I've got some new friends who I think will be able to help him. We're going to meet them all very soon.'

The friends were Jehovah's Witnesses. I liked them. They were nice, kind people. Two of them came round to the flat and were trying to look serious while lolling on the leopard-skin floor cushions in our living room. Not many people could have pulled that one off. Bless them, the super-serious Witnesses failed totally. I was at one end of the sofa, sitting on my dad's knee, while Mum sat totally upright at the other. Even then, I could read a mood and sense an atmosphere. I could tell that Mum was nervous and that Dad was somewhere else.

The Witnesses were both very smartly dressed. They looked a bit like staff in a bank. They talked quietly and intensely for what felt like a lifetime. I wanted them to leave, of course. All I wanted to do was play with my dad. But something about my mum's face told me that all this talk was important, and something about the way Dad had been acting told me he was in no mood to have fun.

Although I was over the moon to have Dad back, he'd become more and more moody, locking himself in the bathroom and not coming out for ages. His mates had scared me too. I'd not really registered the fact that Dad had never brought friends round to the flat before. But this time there had been a stream of strangers, none of whom seemed to even notice that I was there.

Mum told me once that I'd been a people pleaser since the day I was born. I'd never had that many friends of my own age, plus I was an only child, so I was always happy trying to entertain adults. I'd sing or dance or try to tell jokes and do impressions. I did a great Margaret Thatcher, though I say so myself. But my favourite was doing the Queen. I reckoned I had the voice and the wave down perfectly. I'd smile and play, hold anyone's hand, sit on anyone's knee and be happy being looked after by absolutely anybody. What I didn't like was being ignored. Dad's friends walked right by me and looked right through me. One of them, a young, skinny black guy with a thick beard, spent a night on our sofa. His mouth was wide open as he slept and when I crept past him in the morning I was mesmerised by his gold teeth.

'Who's that, Mummy?' I asked in the kitchen.

'He's nobody,' she said. 'He'll be gone soon. But let's not wake him.'

I remember we ate breakfast in my room that morning. It was a treat, but it was strange. We'd had men with safety pins in their noses sleeping on our sofa before and Mum had just woken them up and tipped them on to the floor with a smile if she wanted room for me and my breakfast. I couldn't work out why this man was different. He was wearing white trainers rather than big black punk boots. Surely that made him a child, like me. I didn't think he could be scary at all.

Mum said later the idea behind having the Witnesses round had been for them to give Dad a new path to follow. She wanted him to listen and find some kind of direction. But Mum was already interrupting and asking questions. 'So what happens to our souls when we die?' she was saying. She couldn't help herself. I slipped off my dad's knee so I could cuddle up to his side. That way I could look him in the eye as well. Maybe if I thought really hard, I could get him to take me out for the rest of the day. Maybe he would take me to McDonald's for my tea. I soon realised that Dad wasn't reading my thoughts. He seemed to be struggling to stay awake and I suddenly thought that was the funniest thing ever. I was bored out of my mind too. Why did all these people just want to talk all the time?

'Sit still, Ash.' At least my mum had noticed me. Being told off was better than being ignored. But the afternoon dragged on and on. By the end, I saw a familiar look in my mum's eye. I acted all polite and said goodbye to the Witnesses the way I knew Mum wanted me to do. But I was sure we would be seeing them again. I could tell that she was already hooked.

Religion made Mum strong. Belief and faith got her through things, fired her up, gave her even more energy than normal. It also made her feel safe. When she was on a spiritual path, she could focus totally on the future. The past didn't matter. In fact, the sooner she moved away from the past, the better. So when Dad disappeared again, not long after she started to get involved with the Witnesses, she took it all in her stride. Years later, she told me it was a drugs offence that took Dad back to prison that time. He told me it was for some other thing and that drugs came later. Either way, it was just me and Mum in our Kentish Town flat again – me, Mum and our new religion.

She read so much and she learned so fast. I was her first convert. I didn't have any choice in that. Mum loved that being a Witness made things very clear. There were rules, structures, right and wrong. Then there was the big clock ticking, counting down to the end of the world, when everyone gets judged. That meant Mum had to act fast to put things right. She had to make sure we were in a good place if Judgement Day arrived. So she made her big decision: to protect me and my future, she would walk away from every single aspect of her past life. She believed Dad was a bad influence, and her plan was that he must never find us again. She would leave her friends and her family. She would leave her business. We would both leave our home.

'What's going on, Mum?'

I'd just got back from a friend's flat and the hall was full of black bin-liners, suitcases and bags.

'Nothing, Ash, love. I'm just cleaning up and throwing some things out.'

My bedroom door was open and the room looked bare. All my toys and dolls were gone. The sheets and duvet were off my bed. It was the same in Mum's bedroom, and our living room was just as empty. It all looked as if we'd died.

'Shhh, Ash. We're going on a trip. But not just yet.' Mum looked at her watch. 'I need to ring them and then they'll be here any minute.'

At first, I thought 'they' would be the Witnesses. But it wasn't them. Two men finally came up our stairs. They were nice, but they were strangers. 'Is that everything? Don't you want to take any more of the furniture?' one of them asked my mum when all the bags and cases had gone. She shook her head, which I didn't understand. Why would she not want all her lovely things?

Down on the street I was cold and my bottom lip was trembling. Mum pushed me into the front of a big white van. She was looking all around us and was in a mad hurry to get going. 'Are we coming back?' I asked, starting to cry. Mum just held my hand, staring up and down the street as the engine started and we headed out towards Camden High Street. 'Everything's going to be OK,' she said. But nothing would ever be the same again.

CHAPTER FOUR

———————————●———————————

IN HIDING

The van took us less than two miles away, but it might as well have been 5,000, because we climbed out into a completely different world. I stood on the pavement outside the steps of our new home in Cambridge Gate, Regent's Park. It was a palace. Tall, wide and gorgeous, it had a huge, shiny black door with a gold letter box and it was easily the biggest, grandest, most expensive house I had ever seen. The whole street was like something out of a film set. I felt like I was in *Oliver!*, when Oliver wakes up in his benefactor Mr Brownlow's house and realises that his life has been changed. Our new street actually looked just like the one in that scene. Every house was perfect, just as beautiful as the next. They were a lovely brown colour and every one of them gleamed in the night air. Even the lamp posts looked like something out of Disneyland. Little green trees grew out of little black boxes to each side of every door. The pavement was wide and there was no litter, no mess, not even any people. It simply could not have been more different to our old estate in Kentish Town. From that very first moment, I loved the place and I hated it. It was fantasy land, but it scared me. I couldn't help but think that Mum and I would never fit in. We'd never get a happy ending like Oliver.

'This is us, babes,' Mum said, opening the building's big front door so the two guys could start to unload the van. 'This is God blessing us for choosing the right path. This is his proof that we're doing the right thing.' We headed into a hall as wide as the whole of our old flat. Then we went up a vast, curving stairway like something Cinderella would walk down. Our flat was on the second floor. It looked as grand on the inside as it did from the street.

'This is your room,' she said, leading me into a room at the front of the building that looked right out over the road towards the blackness of the park. It was massive. It had vast high ceilings, deep built-in wardrobes and enormous old windows. 'Come and see mine.' Mum was going to sleep in an equally great room at the back. 'This is going to be my sewing room,' she said, waltzing into yet another room down our long, high hall. As we walked around, I completely forgot to be afraid of this incredible new place. Mum's mood had changed as well. She was dancing as she showed the guys where to leave the bags and cases. She gave them some money, waved them off and then ran back to my side.

'What do you think? Better than the old dump?' She bolted our big door closed and let out a big, deep breath. Then we really did do a mad, wild dance. Mum grabbed me and dragged me round the shiny, slippery wooden floors of our new palace, twirling me, dipping me, making me dizzy with excitement. We ended up in a heap in front of the French windows in the living room, just howling with laughter. 'Aisleyne, we are going to be so happy here,' Mum kept saying. It was infectious and wonderful. For that night, I believed her. I was sure she was right.

The following morning, Mum said she needed to talk to me. Because we hadn't brought much with us, we were rattling around our new rooms trying to make the few bits of furniture we'd brought fill the wide open spaces.

We sat down by the front window, looking down over the wide, deserted and unfriendly looking street. My spitfire of a mum started talking very slowly. 'I'm going to find you a new school and this is where we're going to live from now on, Ash. Everything is going to be all right here. But I need you to be very clever and very grown-up because we need to keep everything a secret from Daddy.'

'Why?'

'Because Daddy isn't very well, you know that. People are looking after him and if he gets better he's going to have a new home to go to where he'll be happy. But if he comes to our house here, he might get ill again. That's why no one is going to tell him where we are.'

'So when can I see him again?'

'I don't know, baby. Look, I want you to remember that Daddy is a good man, but the people he has around him aren't. His friends are very bad people and they make him do bad things. If he comes and sees us here, then Daddy and his friends might make us do bad things as well. So we're going to have a new adventure here. We're going to make it on our own, just you and me. We'll make new friends and we'll soon forget we ever lived anywhere else. Maybe you can see Daddy again when you're a lot older. But not till then.'

I didn't know what to say, so I kept quiet. It would be a long time before I realised how deadly serious Mum was about this. Years later, I discovered that she had been to the Citizens Advice Bureau, seen a lawyer and taken out an injunction to stop Dad approaching us while I grew up. Then she had carefully and deliberately cut us off from every aspect of our former lives. She hadn't told her family or a single one of our old friends and neighbours about our move. She'd wanted the removal van to come at night just in case anyone saw us leaving and started asking questions. She hadn't told any of the punks, Goths and hippies who used to come round and she hadn't told any of the fashion crowd either. What I couldn't believe was that she had given up the shop in Kensington Market as well. Phrantik Psycho had been her dream. It was what she had worked for all her life and it was a huge success. But she knew it would be one of the first places Dad would go if he came looking for us. So she had just locked up one night, handed the key to one of the other stallholders and walked away for good. She'd not taken a single piece of stock. She'd given up everything she had ever worked for because she wanted to hide me from my dad. She wanted to protect me from the bad influences of drugs and crime that she said swirled all around him. It took me so long to realise all this. Much too long. The sacrifices that my mum made for me were incredible.

Mum's masterstroke had been finding our incredible new flat. If Dad came looking for us, he might expect to find us in some other council block in Kentish Town; he might ask around the housing association homes in another nearby borough. But the vast houses on the Inner and Outer Circles of Regent's Park? This was where millionaires lived. The street wouldn't even be on his radar.

Mum's new friend Belinda, one of the Witnesses, had helped her find the flat. Belinda was the caretaker of the building. Someone had moved out and we got the place at a bargain rate. 'It's God blessing us,' Mum said again and again as she explained how we had got to live in such luxury. She was convinced it was the ultimate proof that the Jehovah's Witness faith paid off.

We lived above two gay guys who seemed to spend half the year in America and a rich Arab family who we hardly ever saw. That suited my mum just fine – the last thing she wanted was nosy neighbours asking too many questions.

And it wasn't as if we were on our own. Mum might have ditched all her old friends, but she had an army of instant replacements in the wings. The Witnesses were ready to help their own. They came round every day, in huge groups, to settle us in. All credit to them, they were the kindest people alive. Their actions were what religion should be about: helping those in need and not asking for anything in return.

Day after day, they brought us new things, practical, useful gifts like pans and pillows. They made it all seem like an adventure. One of the men brought a guitar and most nights we'd sing songs while Mum cooked huge bowls of pasta or made vegetarian lasagnes, which we would eat lolling around on the floor, looking like a bunch of disciples, I guess.

Before long, we got to work on the flat itself. I saw a spark light up my mum's eyes as the paint pots came out. Every room ended up a different colour. My bedroom was like the seaside. I had shiny, varnished wood floors; the walls were beach yellow and my ceiling was a sky, with fluffy white clouds instead of the stars I'd had at the old flat. Our vast living room had metallic gold skirting boards and window frames. We had a huge five-foot fireplace, which Mum also painted gold. It gleamed at night, just the way she knew it would. We had blue walls and Mum found some big, round wicker chairs, which sat by the French windows. She picked silver and pink for the hall, and it looked fantastic. Her room had a Moroccan theme – again, years ahead of the trend. She created a sort of tent structure made out of thin pastel-coloured muslin and covering the whole ceiling. Her walls were rich warm russets and golds. It was exotic and wonderful. I was going through a real princess phase again and I loved the romantic feel of Mum's room.

Less than a month or so after moving in, Mum and I had the most extraordinary place to call home. 'We don't need a garden,' Mum would say, flinging open our huge French windows on sunny days, 'we've got the whole of Regent's Park to play in.' We still danced around our big rooms sometimes, full of joy about our fresh start. We even made some friends, not among the millionaires or the bankers or the rich foreigners in the other Regent's Park mansions but at a squat just down the road. They had a brilliant party just after we moved in. Everyone was dressed up as aliens and spaceships and planets. It might have been a squat, but the flat was as well decorated as ours – Mum had found people just as creative as her. The sofa there was a giant set of red lips. I loved it. We also hung out at the nearby Diorama Theatre. I watched films and plays, saw rehearsals and did workshops, and met some brilliant new people. One day, Mum bought a huge chessboard of a carpet and put it down in our living room. A friend of hers taught me how to play using massive plastic pieces that were nearly as big as me. I even had ballet lessons from a gorgeous teacher who called me 'Miss Aisleyne'. That always made me feel like a princess. Mum and I were only a few miles from our old home but it was so totally different from life back in Kentish Town. Sometimes whole days would go by without me thinking about my dad at all.

CHAPTER FIVE

KNOCKING ON DOORS

With no shop to design for and run, my mum needed something else to fill her days. She found it in her new religion. During our first few months in Regent's Park, the Witnesses came round all the time; they pretty much held meetings in our living room. But the proper meetings took place in Kingdom Hall, as the Witnesses call their places of worship. We started to go all the time. Then we hit the streets and started knocking on doors.

When you are in the ministry – in other words, when you're actively involved with the Witnesses and going out spreading the word – you have to dedicate a certain number of hours to the cause each week. For Mum and me, that meant three main meetings and a lot of time out pounding the pavements. On Tuesdays and Sundays, we went to Kingdom Hall up in Camden Town, on Pratt Street. Those were two-to-three-hour meetings: a bit of prayer and some songs, then an hour or so of serious talk, then some more relaxed chat. Much of the talk time was filled with readings from *The Watchtower* and detailed question-and-answer sessions. Even though I was normally bored out of my mind, I could get the message. I could also see why Mum stuck to this faith, although she'd given up on so many others. The whole story was based on facts, not just blind faith. That meant that the Witnesses could answer Mum's questions. When she needed more information, they could provide it. When it came to religion,

Mum followed her head, not her heart, and this faith made sense to her.

For me, the Thursday meetings were the ones to look forward to. Most of them were held in other Witnesses' homes. We went all over London and I got to nose around a bit if I said I needed to be excused to go to the bathroom or if I offered to help with the food and drinks. I loved looking around other people's houses. I wanted to see if anyone else was as creative as my mum. No one ever was. Better still, at lots of these meetings I started to meet a few other kids my own age. Over in Bayswater, there was one cool black girl called Michelle, who got away with a lot more than I did and always had a funny story to tell. We were friends for ages. In Shepherd's Bush, I met two black brothers called Jean-Michel and David who were French and seemed really exotic. I'd had my first-ever crush way back at nursery school, on the teacher, a Bob Marley lookalike with the most wonderful hair I'd ever seen. Then there was little Caleb at junior school, who lent me the laces from his skates one day when mine broke. That was love, right? But Jean-Michel and David were my first proper crushes. I didn't meet anyone my own age in Regent's Park – I hardly ever even saw any other kids in the posh houses – so Witness meetings filled that gap.

The Witnesses were a total mixed bag. Maybe that's why Mum and I fitted in. White, black, Chinese and Irish people dominated, but there were so many other nationalities and types as well. Some of the Witnesses were clearly super-rich. Many were really poor. We had one woman with Tourette's syndrome. She was fine when she was taking her medication, but she went wild when she forgot. 'Fuck, fuck, fucker, toilet, wanker, fuck!' she would scream in the middle of meetings. She was my favourite – until a mad lady joined and started to disrupt meetings by getting her kit off in front of us all. Even this seemed tame compared to one of the others, though. This guy was nice and normal for months on end. Then he'd disappear for a few weeks and arrive back at Kingdom Hall head to toe in black leathers screaming obscenities at everyone and saying he would kill us all. The meetings with him were so exciting I didn't even have to pretend to need the loo three or four times an hour just to pass the time.

Missing out on Christmas and birthdays was the other big change after we became members. As I got used to that part of the faith, it wasn't the presents I missed (well, not much). What I did miss was the fun of Christmas. I hated having to sit out Christmas assemblies and all the parties. I hated going back to school in January and not being able to join in when everyone else talked about what they'd got and what they'd done. In the old days, in our crazy Kentish Town flat, we always had huge parties with Mum's fab friends. We sang punk versions of carols, sometimes with me bashing out the tune on my tiny little black plastic piano. Mum and I always had the biggest tree on the block and the brightest, boldest decorations. Each year, Mum designed something special for our door and windows. Between us, we created amazing wreaths and built beautiful snowy scenes to cover every surface in our flat. It was all that artistry that I missed in the Witness years, all the creativity Mum had shown and all the fun I'd had sharing it. But it wasn't as if Mum and I didn't have things to do together in our new world. When you're in the Witnesses, you always have a job to do.

'Hello, we're here with *The Watchtower* and *Awake!*. Can we take a few minutes of your time to talk about our faith?' Going out on the streets to try and convert people was the very worst part of my mum's new world. Hated it, hated it, hated it. I'd try anything to get out of it. I don't feel well. I've hurt my foot. I'm tired. I've got a cold. I've got flu. I've got a huge spot on my nose. Nothing ever worked. Summer or winter, rain or shine, we headed out with our A–Z and our stack of magazines. Twice a week, we did our two-hour sessions, first with other Witnesses to see how they approached it, then, for years, on our own. Twice a week, for two hours, we took all the abuse people threw at us. Just for knocking on a door or ringing a bell and saying a few polite words, we would be sworn at, physically pushed into the street, spat at, or all three. For interrupting *EastEnders*, we would be treated like scum. (I never understood that at the time. Today, I sort of have to admit I see those people's point. I won't even answer the phone when *EastEnders* is on, so don't even try knocking on my door.)

If the assaults in the street were bad, then the times we got invited into people's homes could be worse. Yes, Mum and I had some lovely times, when we met charming, lonely people who welcomed any chance to talk to someone new. There was one old guy who made us lunch and showed us photos of his late wife. I wished he was my grandad. Then there were the millionaires in Notting Hill and Holland Park who led us through vast houses so we could pitch to their spiritual sides. There were some fiercely clever young people who just seemed to like the idea of getting into some big debate. Most of the time I reckon they regretted it. They might have been to Oxford or Cambridge, but my mum could eat their arguments for breakfast. There was never anything they could say that she couldn't answer. Sometimes we even got the message across and persuaded a few people to join us for meetings and take on the faith. It might only have happened with one person in a thousand, but that person was the reason we went out there.

That was why we also spoke to all the nutters and the misfits. My theory is that deranged people whose houses stink of piss are most likely to invite a Jehovah's Witness in for a cuppa. They are also the least likely to let you leave in a hurry. I remember this crazy guy who had box after box of rubbish stacked up in an overheated living room. In one eerie house in Acton, there wasn't a single chair, but the guy pulled out cardboard boxes full of chewing gum and Lucozade for us to sit on. He let my mum talk for ages and then offered me a drink. When I said I'd have a Lucozade, seeing as I was sitting on a box containing 12 bottles of it, he said it was evil and he didn't have any! What a weirdo. Over time, we stopped being fazed by the people with filthy clothes and the ones who had cat poo in plastic bags on the floor, by the creepy old pervs who scratched their balls, wanted to show me where the bathroom was in person or never took their eyes off me all the time we were in their house. Turning up on the doorstep of someone who believed in another religion could be tough as well. Mum and I got involved in too many rows when people tried to turn the tables and convert us to some other faith before we could try and sell the Witnesses to them.

But despite the bad experiences, my mum was hooked on the whole thing. She was determined to get others to see what she saw in the faith. She said it had saved her, changed her whole life for the better. She wanted others to feel the same. Slowly, as her old confidence came back, so too did her creativity. Her punk days were over, but she began to make funky clothes for some of the Witnesses. She bought a new desk to design on and then she started to apply for jobs. I had gradually begun to think about my dad again. Mum and I still rattled around in our big flat and didn't really fit in among the neighbours. Suddenly, though, it looked like everything was going to be all right.

'Ash, you've got to listen to this!' Mum said, grabbing me one afternoon as I came in from junior school. She was beaming with excitement. I loved it when she was like that.

'We're calling to say we enjoyed meeting you, we very much like your work and we'd like you to call as soon as you can to discuss a full-time position here.' Mum was hopping from foot to foot as she played me the answerphone message. It was from a company called Promise that supplied Topshop with designs. Mum was back in business. Someone else had finally spotted how talented she was. Suddenly, we were arm in arm, dancing around our living room the way we had the night we first arrived in the flat. We fell over, laughing, just as we had back then. A job like this had to be the start of something good. I loved Topshop. How cool that my mum would be part of it. She could get me free samples, right? And a big staff discount?

The design studio was up in Gospel Oak, north London, and I would have visited every day if they'd let me. It was a big, buzzing place and everyone there was passionate about fashion. The company did photo shoots up there sometimes and I was mesmerised by the sleek, gorgeous models who stood around all day having half-made clothes pinned to their bodies. I liked the photographers, who wore leather jackets and were always chewing gum, and I loved the wildly camp men who did everyone's hair and make-up and made a fuss of me when they had time.

But at the heart of it all were the designs. Mum had a huge desk in her own office. I'd sit at one side of it and watch her work on dress patterns, do her cuttings, look through the vast choice of fabrics and samples. When she was happy with her first version, we'd move to the machinists and watch them do their magic downstairs. I sat with them for hours, watching and learning, trying to work out how they could move their hands so fast and sew so straight.

Mum's boss was a power-dressed woman who let me use her private bathroom when I needed to go to the toilet. I probably asked to go up to four times an hour some days – but it wasn't because I needed to pee. I went because Mum's boss had a huge bottle of Poison on the shelf next to all her expensive little scented soaps. It was so rich, so cloying; I adored it. I sprayed myself with it on every visit to the toilet, never understanding that when it comes to super-strong perfume less really is more.

Away from work, Mum was finally getting to relax as well. She was earning good money so bills weren't quite as stressful as they used to be. She started cooking amazing meals again. She went back to making those huge vegetarian lasagnes and casseroles – aubergine and red kidney beans, courgettes and garlic cloves. That winter, Mum and I learned to laugh again. Our flat was freezing cold. The huge, high rooms cost a fortune to heat and, as Mum was using up most of her salary to repay debts, we didn't have the spare cash to spend on gas. We had a little Calor gas heater and at night we slept curled up together on a sofa bed in the hallway. Now, when I say 'hallway', remember this was Regent's Park, so it was big enough to be called a room in itself. It was the warmest place in the flat because it didn't have any windows. It was like camping. It was as if we were squatters in our opulent millionaire's mansion.

We giggled and told stories and enjoyed our life. I remember when we heard thunder one night, Mum told me, 'That's just God moving the furniture around.' I even forgot that I thought the house was haunted. Since we'd moved in, I'd been convinced I had heard a woman in stilettos walking up and down our hallways. I was sure I'd seen floating figures and heard weird mumbling in the night, and I reckoned I'd seen mist coming up from under the spare-bedroom door one time. I went through a phase when I wouldn't even go and make Mum a cup of tea because I was too afraid to head down to the kitchen on my own. But as we nested in the hall that first winter, I wasn't afraid any more. We were mum and daughter against the world. It felt great, and for a while it kept on getting better.

Mum was still good friends with Belinda, the Witness who had helped her find the flat. Belinda was half-English, half-Indian and stunningly beautiful. When Mum met her, she owned a vintage clothes shop in Kentish Town. Then she moved out of London and set up a shop hiring out ball gowns in Oxford. To me, still obsessed by princesses, it was heaven on earth. Could anything be better than that place? Everything in Belinda's shop was lovely and beautiful; it was a treasure trove of silk and taffeta and sparkling diamanté. I would examine every inch of the clothes, trying to work out how they were made. I loved the willowy blonde students who came in, with their long legs and incredible confidence. I wanted to have that kind of poise one day. Sometimes I'd practise trying to walk the way they did. Don't think I ever really pulled it off!

Belinda had two children, India and Paris, who seemed just as glamorous as her. I adored having them as friends. When summer came, we all went punting, had picnics and lived like something out of an old Hollywood film – not least because Mum had just bought herself a red BMW, so even our journeys to and from Oxford were the last word in cool.

Then there was Mum's other best friend, a fashion buyer called Rose. She wore summer dresses and was blonde, glamorous and, compared with Mum, conventional. Rose lived in an amazing flat in Maida Vale, where she cooked wonderful curries. We ate them by candlelight at a proper table with place mats and coasters. She played Bobby Brown's album *Don't Be Cruel* all the time and we would dance round her flat. I loved Rose.

I think I liked all this so much because I was going through a tiny bit of an *Absolutely Fabulous* phase. I was the prim and proper Saffy, and I wasn't thrilled that my mum had always been Edina. I wanted to live like Belinda and Rose, with their floaty clothes and posh dinner parties. Instead, back in Regent's Park, Mum served vast meals to an endless stream of people who just took their plates and lounged around on huge floor cushions while they ate. I wanted a three-piece suite and a dining table. I wanted coffee tables and standard lamps. I wanted things that matched. Instead, we got more Americana, retro furnishings and arty kit from canal-side markets, all of which I bloody love now, but it wasn't what I liked at the time. I just wanted to be 'normal', like the other kids at school. Today,

I realise that there's no such thing as normal, but in those days it was what I longed for.

But I did have confidence. I fed off my mum's good mood and got the feeling that nothing was impossible. I started putting on pretend radio shows in my bedroom. I played music, introduced imaginary guests, even handed out prizes in made-up competitions. I thought I was good at it. I thought I might have a future as an entertainer. Then I read an article about stage schools in some girls' magazine. Who didn't dream of a life like the kids from *Fame*? I became obsessed with following in their footsteps. 'Mum, please can I go to Sylvia Young?' I used to whine about it all the time.

Mum was up for it. She called them and got me an audition. The only thing she didn't tell me was that I was supposed to have prepared a set of routines. I didn't know that I would be the only applicant wearing a bright-green leotard, either. The only music I had in my bag was a tape of the Teenage Mutant Ninja Turtles. So when my turn came to take to the stage, that was all I had to work with. Routine? What routine? I did the running man on the spot, mortified. I kept on running for the full four minutes. At one point, I decided to switch it up a bit and turn around. I was still doing the running man on the spot, but this time the judges could see me doing it from the side and the back (like that would clinch it!). As I turned my back to them, I screwed my whole face up in embarrassment. Then I saw that the stage was surrounded by mirrors. The judges had seen me do it. What's more, while all the other kids had been sleek and professional, in what they did and what they wore, when I saw myself in the mirror I looked like a giant, scared turtle on speed. No wonder I hate auditions to this day.

'Why didn't you tell me I needed music and dance clothes?' I bawled at Mum, crying my eyes out, as we walked back through Regent's Park to our flat. 'Everyone else had proper routines and I looked like an idiot.'

'Ash, if you were supposed to get into that school, then you would have got in without any practice,' she said. 'Everything happens the way it happens. There's a reason for everything and we can't fight that.'

'But you fought to get your shop in Kensington.'

That was 'different', of course, though Mum couldn't tell me why. What she did do was find me some dance classes so that I would be better prepared for any future auditions. While I never did get to go to Sylvia Young full time, I did do a few summer-school courses over the next couple of years. I was starting to feel ambitious.

Meanwhile, the Saffy in me was banished for a while when I was reminded that I should be proud of my brave, wild mum, not embarrassed by her. At school in Primrose Hill, I had finally started to make friends, and it seemed they all loved my mum. One of my closest friends was a girl called Louise. One afternoon, we found a deep crack at the edge of the playground. For some reason, we started digging. 'Let's dig right through to your house, Ash,' said Louise. 'Then I'll bring all my stuff to school and we can escape there. I can live with you and your mum forever.' She wasn't the only one who thought Regent's Park was a haven. My mate Alison also said she would rather live with my mum than hers.

Then there was another of our classmates. She was always showing us bruises, saying that her mum had hit her the night before. One time, we went to her house and all sat in the lounge, terrified, when her Mum turned on her and started screaming at her and beating her in the bedroom.

'Why don't you use your sheets as a rope and climb out of your window one night?' I said. 'Then you can come and live at mine with Louise and Alison.' When I said it, I meant it. Because life at home was happy – and I'm sure my mum would have welcomed any number of waifs and strays into our world. She was confident, creative and inspired again. I loved her. I felt as if almost all of the pieces in life's jigsaw were coming together. I was sure we could put together a perfect picture – if we could only slot in one last missing piece: my dad.

CHAPTER SIX

●

UNDER ATTACK

In five years, Mum and I had seen Dad only once, and that was totally by chance. I'd have been about ten. We'd been to Oxford for the day and had run out of petrol in Camden, less than ten minutes from our front door. 'There's a petrol station over in Parkway. We'll have to walk,' said Mum.

I didn't even recognise Dad until Mum pointed him out to me. 'That's your Dad over there,' she said the moment we walked onto the forecourt. He was climbing out of a white Porsche, wearing a short-sleeved white shirt with the buttons open halfway down his chest. He had a huge gold chain round his neck, but, unlike some of the huge chains you see today, his looked classy. It might have been an antique Indian one. He gave me one of those years later and I treasured it. What his chain told me was that my dad was ahead of the trend. He was wearing that sort of thing years before it became fashionable and even more years before it became naff. No wonder he'd caught my mum's eye from the start. They were two peas in a pod, just with different ideas about style. He had some blonde girl sitting beside the car while he was washing it and there were two massive pit bull dogs running around them both. It had been so long since I'd seen him. He had put on some weight but there was no doubt it was him. I was stunned, shocked, scared, nervous.

'Mum?' I asked, as we froze on the pavement. Should we carry on or walk away? Wasn't this what I had wanted for so long? Wasn't it what Mum had feared? I don't think either of us knew how to handle the situation. So Mum took control.

'Come on. We're just going to get the petrol and go,' she told me. 'He's fat,' she said as we got closer. 'Call him "Fatty Daddy". Remember that he cares more about those two dogs than he ever has about you.'

Looking back, I can see that she reacted like that because she was really hurt and humiliated to see him there with his fancy car and his new girlfriend while we walked up with our empty petrol can. And I'd never have said anything nasty in a million years if at that exact moment I hadn't seen his girlfriend look at us and laugh. The bitch. I suddenly felt I had to defend my mum. How dare this stranger mock us? She had no idea how strong my mum was.

'Fatty Daddy, Fatty Daddy,' I sang out like a little baby as we walked past him. He just stared at his car and didn't look at us. He didn't say a single word. Not to me, not to Mum, not to his girlfriend. He finished washing his car and we filled up our little red petrol can. He and Mum went into the kiosk separately to pay and I stood on the little concrete platform between the pumps trying to pretend I wasn't looking at the blonde woman and the dogs. Then it was over. No goodbye, no wave, nothing. The Porsche made a huge amount of noise as it powered into the main road and headed north towards Hampstead. Then Mum and I walked back to our own car and headed home. Neither of us spoke for ages. Then we just started talking about our day out in Oxford. It was as if Dad didn't even exist.

Just because Mum didn't talk about Dad to me, didn't mean she didn't talk about him full stop. I listened at a lot of doors as a girl. I think I sensed that people were keeping things from me, so I saw that as a way of regaining some control. The trouble was, I didn't often like what I heard. Mum told terrible stories about my dad to the other Witnesses. I would hear her on the phone to her mates saying he had pushed her, hit her, all sorts of things. She talked about the crimes she said he had committed. She talked about drugs and about what they did to him. For me, that came out of nowhere. It was listening to those conversations that I first heard anyone talk about my dad and drugs. I was totally freaked out by it and couldn't believe it. It painted a picture of a man I didn't know. Mum went on and on about secrets and lies. 'I pushed the bathroom door open once after he had been in there for an hour and he was out cold,' I heard Mum saying once. 'There was silver paper on the toilet seat and matches all over the floor. When he came round, he said he'd been making a doll's house for Aisleyne.' It was years before I realised what that silver paper might have been for. For too long, I loved my dad even more because I thought he really had been making me a doll's house.

It all made me even more determined to get my dad back. I was a huge *Blind Date* fan and I was convinced that I could be a matchmaker, just like Cilla. I could get rid of the blonde girl and get Mum and Dad back together. All I needed to do was find Dad again. I decided that Mum couldn't possibly have covered all our tracks. Dad must be able to find us, if he wanted to. I no longer saw him as a superhero but I knew he wasn't stupid. I knew the silly song I'd chanted at the petrol station must have hurt him, but I was still certain that he would want to make contact again.

One night Mum and I came home from a meeting at Kingdom Hall and both thought Dad had found us. We climbed the building steps, went in the big black door and then spotted something frightening. The door to the gay guys' flat below us had been hacked open. The whole bottom half of it was missing. What was left was hanging ajar.

'Are you in there?' Mum called, knocking. We rang the bell, but no one replied so we hovered on the threshold. We were terrified. In the end, we went in. It was as quiet as the grave. Suddenly, living in such a big building didn't seem like a good idea. Were our other neighbours in? Would anyone hear us if we screamed? 'Hello? Michael? Martin?' We edged into their living room. It was dark, dusty and empty.

'Your dad must have broken in,' Mum said, suddenly. 'He's found us. He's just got the wrong flat.'

Overwhelming, inexplicable fear, excitement, panic. I'd always been looking for Dad, watching out for him on the street whenever I was out, but I'd started looking even harder after the petrol station incident. I'd even devised a plan with a friend at school to go knocking on all the doors in Kentish Town until I found him. I'd wanted to say sorry for calling him names. In this strange, empty flat, did I really want to find him? Would he be a hero or would he let me down yet again? Would he be with the blonde woman? Why the hell would he be hiding in here?

'The bathroom,' Mum said, bringing back awful memories. I was terrified. Surely she didn't think he would cut himself again?

'Which door?' I asked. The flat had a totally different layout to ours. We opened the doors to the bedroom, hall cupboard and kitchen before finding the bathroom. It was empty. No knives, no blood, no Dad.

'If he's been here, then he's gone again,' Mum said.

'So where are Michael and Martin? What's going on?'

To this day, I've never found out. Our neighbours never came back. I have no idea what happened to all their stuff. There was a lot. They had a shiny, black, full-size grand piano, as well as chandeliers in every room. Maybe they moved full time to their place in Florida. Maybe they were ill or dead or in prison. It could have been anything.

'Why didn't they even say goodbye?' I asked Mum. 'That was really nasty of them.' Then I realised that we'd not said goodbye to anyone back in Kentish Town, so I shut up. We've all got our reasons for what we need to do, even if no one else understands them at the time. We went up to our own flat and the door had been kicked in. The fear was even more intense now. The unknown always seemed to shadow my life. Now, behind our broken door, what was there? Was it Dad? We went in, hand in hand, hearts in mouths. But there was nobody there. Stuff had been picked up and put down in different places, but nothing had been taken.

The shadow of the break-in hung over Mum and me for a long time. Mum was convinced it was Dad who had broken in. Who knows if it was him? Whether it was or not, his spirit was certainly in the air. I saw Mum get more worried and nervous day by day. I couldn't get him out of my mind. And more weird things kept on happening.

At Kingdom Hall one time, someone came in to find me. They said my dad was outside if I wanted to go and see him, but when I went outside there was no one there. Another time, we came home from a meeting and a Porsche like Dad's was at the end of the street. It zoomed off and all I saw was a big mass of curly blonde hair and a big hand waving at me.

Then came final proof that Dad still loved me. It was Christmas and outside our door one day was a little Rupert Bear picture book. Being honest, it was way too young for me. It would probably have been a better choice for a little boy. But I loved that book. Dad had written across the front cover: 'To my princess Aisleyne, happy Christmas, love from Daddy, xxx.' For months, it was the last thing I looked at every night, the first thing I touched every morning. It made me feel close to the man I loved. I read it from cover to cover, over and over, as if it would somehow bring me closer to him or give me a clue as to where to find him. He was in my mind all the time. He was still the missing piece in the jigsaw of my life. The book helped fill the gap.

No prizes for guessing that all this freaked my mum out. That was when fate stepped in and gave her something else to concentrate on. We got an eviction notice. It bothered Mum that Dad knew where we were, but she had no intention of being forced out of her home and she fought tooth and nail for us, all by herself. How she did it, I'll never know. She always worked well when there was a cause to focus on. 'Aisleyne, they can't do this to us. We're protected tenants,' she declared, all ready to fight. 'I'm not going to let them get away with this.' So out came a new set of notebooks as she wrote out points of law from reference books. She met up with advisers and lawyers. She was strong again and wasn't obsessed with avoiding Dad any more. I rejoiced.

Better still, we were rehoused while the case went on and I absolutely loved our new place. It was on Albany Street, not far from Cambridge Gate. From our new back windows, we could actually see our old building. What I loved was that this was an ordinary block on an ordinary street full of ordinary people. Walking up to that front door, I didn't feel like a fraud or a fish out of water. I felt comfortable. Our new place was modern and easy to heat and clean. I wanted to stay there for ever and live a normal life. I wanted my dad to find me there, just as he had done at our last flat.

Mum had other ideas, though. She wanted us to emigrate to Australia. 'It'll be amazing, Ash,' she said. But I hated the idea. Sure, I watched *Neighbours*. Yes, I was sort of in love with Jason Donovan and I wanted to be a car mechanic like Charlene. But Australia? I'd made some good friends at school and I'd got over my fear of never fitting in (well, nearly). I was tired of running. Plus, I knew that if we did leave the country, Dad would never find us. I couldn't risk that.

Mum did all the forms and the interviews with the visa people. She threw herself into the challenge like she threw herself into everything else. Her skills as a designer swung it for her. She got the green card, or whatever it was called, and we were ready to go. I stopped her. Or, to be totally accurate, she stopped because of me. When I told her how miserable I'd be if we left Britain, she gave up that dream. It's only now that I see what a massive thing that was. She'd given up her family, friends and Phrantik Psycho to protect me when we'd left Kentish Town. Now she was giving up a new start in Australia for me. Maybe if we'd gone, she would have been saved. Maybe all the problems that came afterwards would have been avoided. Maybe we'd still be together, mum and daughter against the world. Maybe. I can't know. But to this day, I can hardly breathe with the guilt if I think about it too much.

Not long afterwards, I started to have problems at school. Like loads of naturally clever, confident people, my mum didn't have much time for schools. She didn't seem to think homework mattered, at least not as much as my friends' parents did. When I got bad reports, she got angry, of course, but she thought everything I needed to know would somehow sink in further down the line. And because we'd been planning on moving to Australia, my name hadn't been put down for secondary schools. For a while, it looked like I would slip through the cracks. I wanted to go to Camden Girls or to the main school on Haverstock Hill in Hampstead, where most of my friends from primary in Primrose Hill had gone. No way, said Mum:

too close to Dad and his family. Some of the other schools a little further away were already full, so in the end I headed over to North Westminster. To be fair, it wasn't so bad at first. But as term had already begun before my application got approved, I struggled to make friends straight away. And because I didn't live close by, it never got any easier.

Even the good things I tried to do backfired. One girl, Kelly, was being pushed around all the time. The bullies called her 'Smelly Kelly' and made her cry. So one day I tried to stick up for her. I shouted out that people shouldn't be so nasty. I got the shock of my life, because Kelly then decided to turn on me. She called me nasty names just for getting involved. She said she didn't want my help. She ended up on the side of the bullies and they all ganged up on me. How the hell did that happen? I could never work out what I had done wrong. I did have one good mate, Alice, but she hardly ever came to school because of her own family problems. I didn't have many people to talk to, so I became a bit of a daydreamer. I imagined things, planned out different plot lines for my life and tried to while away the days. My biggest dream was that one day Dad would be waiting for me at the school gates. I thought that if he turned up, he would look so cool, big and strong that everyone would want to be my friend.

Something else happened at that school. When I was in the second year, I was jostled along a corridor by a group of boys. They were pack hunting. I was surrounded, pushed and held up against a wall. They were laughing, feeling me up, doing worse. How did they think they'd get away with it? When they took their hands off my mouth and ran, I screamed. In the headmistress's room, I broke down, and she realised something was very wrong. My reaction was too severe, even for this incident. She guessed there had to be something else.

So it all came out: the time at a friend's house, years ago, when her uncle had felt me up under the kitchen table. He'd been strong, insistent, powerful. I'd frozen in fear. I'd let him do things he shouldn't have done. When I'd got home that day, I'd locked myself in the bathroom and cried. Mum had tried to get me to tell her what was wrong but I'd been too ashamed to tell her. I'd never forgiven myself, never understood it. The headmistress was the first person in all the world I'd told of this. My mum was the second, when she came to the school to get me. And it cut her up so much. She researched the guy obsessively. She found out he'd done it before. She talked about it all the time. She blamed herself. She was angry that I'd been allowed to go to that girl's house in the first place. From then on, she was going to hold me even closer than before.

All I wanted to do was forget and move on. Although the police were involved, the case against the boys didn't go to court because there had been so many of them that I couldn't identify them all. So I switched schools at 13. I thought I'd get a fresh start at the Ellen Wilkinson School for Girls in Ealing. I was wrong. It began with all the same old low-level bullying: being picked on, being mocked a bit, being left on my own at lunch and having no one to sit next to in class. I know everyone gets that at one time or another, but it didn't make it hurt any less. I tried everything to feel less lonely, but I always felt like an outsider. Sometimes I thought I'd never fitted in anywhere: as the girl with the hardcore punk mum, I'd never felt at home among the ordinary kids in Kentish Town; after we disappeared, I certainly didn't feel accepted by the rich kids in Regent's Park, who never even spoke to me. Now, because I'd moved schools and had to travel so far each day, I didn't fit in with the local girls at Ellen Wilkinson either. Mum had become really strict ever since the assault at my old school, and she was so fierce about me coming straight home every day that I couldn't hang out at anyone's home and make friends.

I was one of only three white girls in my class. The other two both left before the end of my first term there – one got pregnant and the other just seemed to give up and disappeared. When they were gone, I bore the brunt of the casual racism of some of my classmates. I was the butt of a lot of jokes and cruel comments. It's easy to assume that only non-white kids experience racism, but I was picked on explicitly because I was white.

Then, one day, things got really serious. It was raining in the morning and I told Mum I needed – absolutely needed – to borrow her favourite yellow polka-dot umbrella. I was starting to develop her fashion sense and had decided that an ordinary black umbrella just wouldn't do. Mum gave in. 'Just don't you dare come home without it,' she told me. After school, I was heading back to West Acton Tube to get the Central Line back to Oxford Circus and then the C2 bus up towards Albany Street as normal when I realised I had left Mum's umbrella in class. 'I've got to go back and get it. You go on. I'll see you tomorrow,' I told the girls I was walking with.

I got the umbrella and headed back to the Tube station, where I daydreamed away while waiting for a train. My little fantasy world was interrupted when I saw an angry-looking person approaching me from the other end of the platform. Was it a boy or a girl? Was it a child or an adult? I couldn't tell. He or she was a mass of messy hair and scruffy clothes, talking away to thin air.

Please don't come and talk to me, I thought. But still the figure approached. It seemed to be a girl.

'Is your name Aisleyne?'

What the hell was this all about? How the hell did she know my name? 'Yes, it is,' I said, too shocked to lie.

Whack! The first blow came out of nowhere. I fell back against a post at the side of the platform. Whack! The second blow pushed me right down onto a bench. Why was I being attacked by a stranger?

'What are you doing?' I screamed. But by now she had picked my mum's precious umbrella off the ground and was raising it up to hit me yet again. It fell apart after a couple of blows. She threw it down. Then she got serious. I was trying to scream out as she reached into her pocket and brought out some kind of sock. I know now that it was full of snooker balls. They smashed into the side of my face. I choked on blood. She hit me again and again. I was on the ground and it was relentless. If I could have breathed through the blood, I'd have been screaming to know who she was and what I'd done, as well as begging her to stop. But I couldn't speak. So instead I said a prayer in my head. 'Dear God, please let this stop. Please can it end. Don't let me die.'

At that exact moment, it did stop. A man came running up the platform towards us and pulled my attacker away. She spat and disappeared. A woman ran up and wrapped me up in her coat. I was taken to hospital and put in a neck brace for months while the doctors tried to repair my face and check up on my skull.

• • •

'Ms Horgan, I would suggest that for your own peace of mind you don't watch this recording.' The judge was speaking to my mother. He thought the images of my attack, caught on CCTV, would be too horrific for her to watch. He was right. Though Mum did watch the tape, she told me she very nearly threw up.

We were there because the police had found my attacker, got me to identify her in an ID parade and then set out a straightforward case against her using the CCTV footage of the assault. I hadn't wanted to go to the police, let alone to court. But the wheels started turning while I was in hospital, and the further down the line we got, the more I felt I had to go on with it. Mum said that if I gave in and refused to press charges, the girl would have won. Violence and bullying would have won. She told me I had to stand up and fight against that. She asked me how I would feel if I did nothing and the next girl my assailant attacked died. The guilt took over and I agreed.

We heard a couple of other witnesses give evidence, then a doctor from the Hammersmith Hospital came to court and said I could have died if my good Samaritan hadn't answered my prayer and ended the assault when he did. My attacker was convicted, as the police had been sure she would be.

During the trial, I finally discovered what the attack had been about. It had begun with a girl from my school – a bully, to be exact. She used words, not blows, to bring people down. She made fun of people; she found their weaknesses and picked holes in them; she made other people laugh at them. All this made it easier for other bullies to move in and take things up a gear. I'd been one of her targets for weeks. I'd got used to the sneers, the comments, the nasty nicknames and the clever cruelties. Then, out of nowhere, I managed to get my own back. I'd walked into a classroom and this girl had made a typical comment at my expense. A reply flashed out of my mouth. I don't remember what was said now, but I remember everyone's reaction. It was somehow the ultimate put-down, a bit of witty, clever, crushing banter. The whole room fell about laughing – at her, not at me. I felt great, and I gained a whole lot of friends and respect too. But at that moment, my card had been marked. The attacker was her cousin, a cousin with a history of violence and mental illness. She'd jumped at the chance to protect her so-called family honour.

It wasn't just their family that was disrupted when my attacker was sent to jail, though. I headed home in my neck brace and began a year-long course of physiotherapy. I was offered counselling, which I didn't think was necessary. Looking back, I was almost certainly traumatised by the attack, though, and of course Mum was very upset by it too.

'If your dad had been around this would never have happened. Your dad would have protected you. You know he would.' That's what Mum had said to me in the hospital as she sat crying at my bedside. I realised I'd never seen her really cry before. Not after a row, not after any of the shit that had happened to us, not ever.

'Why are we in this state? Why is God letting this happen to us?' She would go over and over reasons, meanings, questions. She kept returning to the sexual assault on me at my old school, and the one at my old friend's house – the two things I was desperate to forget. She cried tears of anger. And she kept on asking the same question: why, why, why? To Mum, everything happened for a reason. If she dropped the Bible and it opened at a certain page, then that was an important message. Even little things were significant. If a bus came late or was too full for us to board, it was all part of some bigger plan. So the fact that I had been beaten up had to mean something.

She worried about me a lot after the attack, and she was concerned that I had got back in touch with Dad without telling her.

'You've seen him, haven't you?' she said one day when I came in from school.

'Seen who, Mum?'

'Your dad. You're seeing him behind my back, aren't you?'

I had absolutely no idea where that notion came from. I hadn't known my mum thought like that.

'Mum,' I said, 'I've not seen him since that day at the petrol station. I wish I had.'

That made it worse. It sent her off in a whole new direction. She began talking about Dad all the time. He was this bogeyman, someone out to get me and swallow me up into his big, bad dangerous world.

'If you want to see him, then you can,' she'd say, 'but not while you live in this house.'

Then, one night, she told me: 'You know he's seen you, don't you? He's been watching both of us. He drives round and watches us from his car every night.'

'No, he doesn't. He doesn't even know where we live any more.'

Mum shocked me. 'Well,' she said, 'he was here last night. He drives by every night at six. He'll be out there now, in that white Porsche with the dogs and that blonde in the front seat.'

Though it seemed ridiculous, I still got up to go and look. I couldn't help myself. There was no white Porsche at that moment, but shouldn't I sit there all night in case he came by later? I really believed my dad was watching over me. That made me feel really safe and loved.

At the same time, after so many good years, Mum's job at Promise was becoming less of a passion. As each season passed, she began to feel hemmed in by the high street. Designing mass-market clothes for the likes of Topshop was too constricting for her. She hated conforming to the rules over what could and couldn't be produced. Then, one day, the company closed and she was made redundant. I don't think she even went back to collect her stuff.

Coming after the attack on me, it was a real blow. With more time to worry about me, she became more protective. She asked relentlessly about where I'd been and what I'd been doing, and she still worried about whether I was in touch with my dad. It was exhausting. And one word started to fall ever more frequently from her lips: evil.

CHAPTER SEVEN

———————●———————

EVIL

My dad was evil. Our old life had been evil. The people we'd lived with in Kentish Town had been evil. My new friends at school were evil. Boys were evil.

Mum had always been strict about boys and had gone mad when she found out I fancied Jean-Michel and David, the French boys from one of our early Witness meetings. I'd only been about eight and it was all just a bit of silly fun, but we never went to their house again. It was the same with all my other early, innocent little crushes. Mum swatted my friendships with boys away.

As the years went by, she started to police my world ever more closely. I wasn't allowed out in the evenings and had to promise to come straight home from school. I got to ice skate on a Saturday but only if I went with other Witness kids, and Mum never failed to point out: 'God will be watching.'

He must have blinked when I went out shopping with my aunt Ingrid one day when I was about 14. Over the years, we had got back in touch with most of Mum's brothers and sisters, and even Ingrid had rejoined the scene. She became a bit of a mentor to me. She had an amazing job, helping kids at Barnardo's, and I adored her. She used to take me out all the time; our favourite place to go was the Trocadero in Piccadilly Circus. That was where she bought me my first miniskirt. It was blue and black, ribbed and I loved it. The next day, when Mum saw it, she exploded. She marched me back into town to return it. I was totally mortified when she gave the shop assistants an earful for selling it in the first place.

Of course, Mum was only trying to protect me, and given the attacks on me during my first couple of years at secondary school, it was totally understandable that she wanted to do everything she could to keep me safe. Now, I think that perhaps the more I rebelled against her rules, the more she must have felt they were necessary. But I couldn't see that at the time. Fortunately, I had a few friends at school who could share my frustration. There was Jessie, a girl from a super-strict African family who kept her on a tight leash, hoping she could get to university and take on the world. There was one other Jehovah's Witness girl, and she and I shared stories about how smothered we felt at home. Then I had a couple of Muslim friends who became soulmates too. We related to each other so well.

No surprise that Mum was absolutely adamant that sex before marriage was wrong. That's up there alongside the no blood transfusions thing in the Jehovah's Witness rule book. What she didn't seem to be able to see was that, at 14, I wasn't looking for sex. We might not have had the world's best sex-education classes at school, but I did get the message. The last thing I wanted was to get pregnant. I'd been wrapped up in cotton wool for so long I'd hardly so much as held a boy's hand. All I wanted to do was be a normal teenager and go on a few dates.

So I was thrilled – and terrified – when I got asked out for the first time. I'd been to a party at the Jehovah's Witness social club on the Harrow Road Estate. I was walking home when this guy called David, who wasn't a Witness, offered me a lift with one of his mates. When he asked me out, I was thrilled and I gave him my home number. Big mistake. When he called, my mum passed me the phone and stood staring at me during the whole conversation, which wasn't long – I think I lost the power of speech because of the nerves.

She told me he would ruin my life. 'He will take away everything that makes you special,' she said. 'He is a bad influence. He will take you away from God and Satan will punish you.' I decided it probably wasn't worth asking my mum what she thought I should wear.

I did have to speak to Mum, though, when he didn't call. I had a feeling she might know the reason why. I was right. After he'd called, Mum had rung 1471 and she'd called David back while I was at school.

'I found out what you were planning to do with this boy, so I gave him a piece of my mind.'

'What did you say to him?'

'I just told him what kind of people we are. I told him if he wants to date you, he has to come to the Kingdom Hall first.'

Oh, you just told him that, Mum. How nice. I could practically hear it. She had a way of making people feel four years old if she wanted. The next day, after school, I rang David from a phone box and found out that he'd been totally humiliated. She'd gone on and on, he said. She'd basically told him he was worthless and wrong for me. She'd got religious. She'd got patronising. I'd got dumped.

I couldn't help but resent my mum's attempts to keep me away from boys, especially as some of her arguments were quite extreme. My dad had a brother who was just six months older than me. I'd met him as a kid but couldn't really remember him. My mum kept on saying that Dad might have another young brother that none of us knew about. 'Imagine if you ended up dating your own uncle without realising who he was. You can't risk it, Aisleyne.' However, as far as I could see, that was hardly likely to be a problem, as nine times out of ten it would be a black boy in the class I'd have a crush on.

Gradually, things between us got worse. Mum read my diaries – which freaked me out – and she also read my poetry and wrote comments alongside some of it. Maybe she thought she was helping me, but it the things she wrote just seemed sarcastic, which actually really hurt. One morning, she threw water on my face to get me out of bed for church. She told me that I was too thin and didn't have any shape and that boys wouldn't fancy me. Perhaps it was her way of trying to protect me or she was worried about my health, but it ate away at my confidence. I felt demoralised all the time. It seemed as though she was always criticising me, not praising me for anything, perhaps because I didn't know things she felt I should. But how could I know everything that she knew? I felt like a stupid, silly little girl. The only times I felt good about myself were when I acted out some comedy sketch or repeated something off the telly and made Mum laugh. Her laughter was a sign that I could achieve something in life. But as time passed, that happened less and less. After a while, I probably gave up trying. I felt my spirit was being crushed.

But I didn't give up altogether. I found a tiny bit of freedom by getting a part-time job. Mum's old friend Rose was working as a fashion buyer on Berkeley Square and she saw that Eggison Daniel, the hair salon next door to her company, was looking for a Saturday girl. I got the job and worked every Saturday from 8 a.m. to 6 p.m., sweeping the floors, answering the phones, washing customers' hair. It was a gentlemen's salon and, as we were in the heart of Mayfair, they were all super-posh, super-rich customers. Amazing how small the tips were.

I started off on £12 for the day but after a few months the pay went up to £15. It was pretty lousy, but I needed all the money I could get. Mum wasn't working and she was getting too distracted to worry about practical details like my bus and Tube fares to school. Her focus was on religion and she was always thinking about the big issues. When I looked at her, sitting reading furiously on the sofa at night, I could barely recognise her. When she wasn't reading, Mum was talking. To me, to the other Witnesses. She kept on firing out all those old questions: When, what, how and why, why, why?

I loved her, but our relationship was getting more and more volatile. One minute we were best friends and the next everything that was wrong with our lives was my fault. She even threw Australia back in my face, saying she had only stayed here because of me.

Round and round we both went, fighting the same stupid battles. 'Evil, wicked, stupid,' she would say. And it wasn't just her who said hurtful things; I could be pretty hard on her too. There always seemed to be new ammunition for a fight.

My lovely uncle Billy, who had been a model and a sax player years ago and who I adored, had moved over to Ireland and he'd become seriously ill. Among other things, he had a brain tumour and we had a terrible visit one week when everyone thought he was about to die. I spent ages with Uncle Dennis and he smoked all the time while we hung around in the smoking room in the hospital. When he went back to the ward to check on Billy, I picked up all of his cigarette ends. Nasty, I know! Mum and I were staying with a Jehovah's Witness woman and I snuck into her bathroom to try smoking. I wanted to be near a toilet and on my own in case I threw up, and I wanted to be able to clean my teeth afterwards to hide the smell. I opened the window so the smoke had somewhere to go. I thought I'd covered all my tracks. But I made a mistake. I threw the butts out into the garden. Derhhh! The Witness woman found them and told my mum – who hit the roof and blasted right through it. She was devastated and thought there was something seriously wrong with me. I felt like an evil, devil-worshipping freak; I was just a curious teenager. But for Mum, smoking was just the first step to disaster. It was a sign that my life was on the road to ruin. The whole thing was crazy, because I hadn't even liked it! I hardly smoked again till the tension and boredom in the *Big Brother* house got to me, and after that I was able to give up really easily. But Mum always thought the worst. To me, it seemed as if she had no perspective, no reality, no recognition of how wild she had been in her own childhood.

All I wanted to do were silly teenage things: wearing make-up, getting nice clothes, meeting boys. But as far as Mum was concerned, one thing would always lead right to another. The Witnesses are really big on the end of the world and I found it exhausting that in their world-view everything was always on a down escalator to destruction. Teenage pregnancy, single mothers living on benefits in tower blocks, drink, drugs, terrible disease and, of course, the awful, endless wrath of some all-seeing, ever-angry devil: if the world really was this awful, I could see why Mum was so anxious for me; but I didn't believe the world was all bad.

Then the Witnesses gave my mum a chance to do what she loved again. Marlene, one of her dearest friends in the group, came round to say she was getting married. 'Sophia, will you make me a wedding dress?' It was like flicking on a switch. Mum came alive. It was brilliant. Having a project stopped her thinking about me, about evil and all the other things that were preying on her mind. For nearly a month, she walked on air, elated about and energised by the challenge. The religious books stayed on the floor. Instead, Mum sat up at night with her pattern books and material. She went out looking for the best fabrics. She was full of creativity again, and she made the most amazing dress.

It was an off-the-shoulder creation that fitted her friend like a second skin. Mum had started off by making a full toile to make certain it was the perfect size. Then, for the dress itself, she used the most gorgeous raw organza silk. It was cream, and Mum hand-embroidered tiny pearls all across it. It looked like something out of *Vogue*. Mum hadn't missed a trick. She'd thought about the kind of day Marlene would want to have and had sewn in a dreamlike train for the actual ceremony but made it detachable for the dinner and dancing afterwards. The whole dress was so pretty, so clever, and it blew everyone away on the big day. Mum, as the designer, almost upstaged the bride.

The trouble was that once the dress was finished and the wedding over, I was back to walking on eggshells again, the way kids in unstable homes always do. It's all so concentrated when you're the only child of a single mum. Everything's focused on you. I hated it. I had to try and read Mum's moods all the time.

I kept asking her why she didn't do another dress like the one she'd done for Marlene. I didn't see why she couldn't work from home again, like she had before Phrantik Psycho had come along. Mum didn't get it. 'You want me out at work every day so I can't check up on you?' she fired back. I tried to explain what I meant but I got nowhere. I think that gorgeous wedding dress was the last dress of any kind that my mum ever made. It was such a waste.

All the time, Mum was becoming even more worried about what she thought I was doing. Boys, smoking, bad influences, bad language, all of it. I just had normal teenage urges but to Mum they were evil. Everything had to be black or white, right or wrong, good or bad. And in her eyes I was always on the wrong side of the line. What was worse was that it had to be sorted out fast. Like some other Witnesses, Mum believed that the end of the world was imminent; it was almost time for all our lives to be judged. It felt like our relationship was getting out of control.

I got a new Saturday job, this time at Saxone on Marble Arch in the West End. The job itself was a bit of a nightmare. I was always daydreaming and couldn't be bothered with all the customers who came in just to sit down and try a few things on without any intention of buying. But if we could have lived without customers, it would have been a pretty decent place. I got on well with the girls there. My mate Jessie from school worked nearby and used to meet me most nights after we'd finished. We'd glam up and hang out in the Trocadero. And a bigger party time was coming up. I was doing my GCSEs that summer and everyone at school was talking about how they were going to celebrate when they were over. Then I had my cousin Nico making me jealous with wild stories of all the amazing raves she went to in King's Cross. That whole world sounded so incredible, especially to someone who'd barely been in a pub, let alone a club. I followed Nico's advice and started to upgrade the type of music I listened to, getting into the new craze for jungle. I got even more engrossed in fashion, which I secretly hoped my mum might approve of. I saved up for hair extensions and started to wear lots of make-up.

Mum went ballistic. 'You can't go to those places. You mustn't be tempted by these people,' she kept saying. But I was tempted, all the time. The more Mum tied me down, the more desperate I became to break out of my box. It was that whole thing about forbidden fruit. Of all people, my mum should have known about that.

'Mum, I'm not going to go off the rails. I'm not going to get pregnant or do drugs. I'm not stupid,' I told her. I tried to explain what I wanted to do with my future. I'd got all the details of a college in Hammersmith where I wanted to do media studies. I even planned to combine the course with maths – and if that's not keeping your feet on the ground, I don't know what is. But Mum just would not let up.

Finally, two little rows changed everything for good. The first came when Mum tried to stop me wearing make-up. I was 16 and that just seemed ridiculous. So when she lunged at me to try and wipe my face clean, I pushed her. I shoved her away from me and she fell back against our kitchen wall. It's a tiny thing, but it was the first time I'd ever done anything like that in my life. I don't think I'd ever been even slightly violent before. Fights of all kinds scared me. Anything that reminded me of bullying left me cold. We both froze in shock,

Mum holding on to the kitchen worktop, me edging back towards the door. It felt like a bond between us had been broken and it was the worst thing. I was devastated over what I had done.

The final flashpoint came before school the next day. It was breakfast time but we'd already been rowing for what felt like an hour. We'd been going over all the same ground yet again. The things I couldn't, shouldn't, mustn't do. All things I knew Mum had done when she was my age. All things every other teenage girl in Britain did without a second thought.

'I want to see my dad,' I kept saying.

'If he was here your whole life would be ruined,' she said.

'Well, it can't be worse than it already is. I want to find my dad.'

'If you want to see your dad, you can get out and stay out.'

'Then I'm going to move out.'

My mum just laughed. 'Well, move out. But where do you think you're going to go?'

Of course, I had no idea. 'I'll stay with Nico,' I shouted back at her after a moment.

Again, Mum laughed. 'You can't. She's living in a hostel and she won't want you.'

'Well, I'll find someone else.'

I stormed out of the Albany Street building and headed for the C2 bus to school. I fumed all day and tried to think of clever things to say to Mum when I got home. But when I got there, she was miles ahead of me. She was sitting there, dressed all smartly.

'I've got a list of homeless shelters you can call to see if they might have a bed for the night,' she said. 'I'm sure some of them are nowhere near as terrible as people think. Do you want to call them yourself or shall I help you? I've found out how much they cost as well. You'll need £70 a week for most of them. Remind me how much you get from Saxone, would you?'

I felt as if she was goading me, playing games, launching off on yet another mindfuck. From her point of view, it was probably quite different. She was probably just trying to prove to me that I couldn't move out. But I'd had enough. I wanted to prove that I could. I wasn't going to a homeless hostel, but I was going. I ran into our kitchen and picked up some plastic bags and a roll of black bin-liners. I headed to my room and was about to stuff as many things as possible into the bags. Then I decided I didn't even have time for that. Something told me I had to leave right then, with just the clothes on my back. I turned to my mum and told her I was going.

She just looked at me. 'Aisleyne, you're wicked. You're an evil, evil girl,' was all she could say. Well, maybe I was. But I had to find out. So I walked through the door and didn't look back. Well, not straight away.

CHAPTER EIGHT

●

THE HOSTEL

Where was I going? It was getting dark and I knew I had to think fast. I decided that Mum was wrong. Nico *would* be happy to see me. I was sure she would let me stay. The hostel she was staying in was out east in Dalston and I headed there right away. 'I can't go home, babes,' I told her. 'Can I sleep here tonight?' Nico hugged me and said I could stay as long as I needed to. I'd never been so grateful for anything. I slept like a baby that first night on Nico's floor. I felt like I was doing the right thing, like I was getting my life in gear and the sky was the limit. I didn't think there was anything I couldn't achieve.

Nico's hostel was a brilliant place to be. I felt it was a good environment with strong karma. There was a much older girl called Leonie – I guess you could say she was in charge – and she made sure it all ran well. It was safe, clean and respectable – though it was never dull. A group of really fit black guys hung out there all the time. I had crushes on all of them. Why weren't any of them asking me out? 'They're gay, Ash,' Nico told me, after watching me embarrass myself for about a week. Thanks, babes. Of course, I was mortified that I hadn't worked it out on my own. But you know what? I'd never met a gay black guy before, and it just didn't occur to me that that might be the reason.

The boys were there at a big party we had for Nico's 18th on my second weekend in Dalston. They helped push me towards some other guy I fancied – this time a straight guy – who had great clothes and a killer smile. I'm almost too embarrassed to admit what happened next, but here goes. He offered me another drink and started chatting me up. It was all going great. We were sitting on the sofa, getting ready to swap numbers, when I said, 'I am really sorry about this,' and then leant across him and threw up. I vomited all over him and the floor. I can't even pretend it was food poisoning. I'd just led such a sheltered life that I wasn't used to drink. Funnily enough, the guy was really cool about it and left his number with my cousin. I never called him, though; I was mortified.

I swear it wasn't just being sick on the floor that made me leave the Dalston hostel. I was so happy there and the girls all became good mates, but there just wasn't room for me with Nico in the longer term. So one evening I headed over to my uncle Dennis's place while I worked out my next move. Uncle Dennis lived on the Haggerston Estate in Hackney. I'd not been there for years, but I had his address and Den had told me what bus to get on.

I sat on the lower deck with my whole life in two plastic bags. I got off the bus when I was halfway up the Kingsland Road and looked around me. The big sign with a map of the estate was covered in red graffiti, so I couldn't work out where my uncle's building was. I was heading towards the first big block to try and check its name when I saw the gang. Just in front of the building, there were four guys sitting on a wall, watching me from underneath their hoods. The one furthest away said something and they all laughed. One of them made a show of playing with himself through his jeans and they all laughed again. I was terrified. Why hadn't I come here in the daytime? And why hadn't I waited till Nico was free so she could have come with me? I tried to decide what to do. I had to either walk on past them or walk away. As I tried to get some courage up, three, maybe four more guys joined them. They all had that swagger. Seeing a lost blonde girl walk on to their patch must have seemed like all their dreams had come true.

There was no one around and I felt that if I walked away and turned my back on them, it would be much worse, so I headed towards them, into the estate. As I did so, the guys who'd been sitting on the wall all stood up. As I got closer, they walked towards me, fanning out so some were on my left, some on my right. I was in a concrete jungle of homes where dozens, hundreds of people must live, but there was no one else in sight. I'd told my mum I was old enough for anything, but I wasn't ready for this.

'What are you doing, girlfriend?' said one of the boys, his tongue drifting on to his upper lip as he looked me up and down. Who did he think he was, LL Cool J? 'What's that in your bags?'

'I'm lost. I'm looking for my uncle's flat,' I said, desperate not to sound scared.

'So what's in your bags?'

'Just some clothes and stuff.'

The pack shifted around me. Some of them were in front of me now, some behind. I stopped walking. There was nowhere for me to go. Still there was no one else around. What was it with this estate?

'Well, where does this "uncle" live?' asked another guy. I told him the address.

'Well, we know exactly where that is.'

'Can you show me?'

They all laughed. 'We can show you a lot of things, baby,' said one.

'Just give us your bags,' said another.

So I did. And this gang of hoodies took me to my uncle's flat, carrying my stuff, then headed back to the main part of the estate. 'Later, girlfriend,' they said as they drifted off. It was a bizarre introduction to this next part of my new life. I'd been so ridiculously, childishly scared, but I felt I had passed my first big test. I'd proved my mum wrong: I didn't need to be afraid of everything; not everything in life was bad; not everyone in the world meant me harm. I started to feel fantastic.

Uncle Dennis was a star. Having me in his flat wasn't easy. He was a painter and decorator back then (he works in mental health now and cares for people with drink and drug problems) and his tiny flat was already stuffed with work gear. But more of a problem was the fact that Mum was his sister. He must have felt he was betraying her by taking me in. Fortunately for me, he understood the situation and knew that it had become impossible for me to live with her. 'It's just for a week or so, till I get myself sorted,' I told him that first evening. 'I'll get myself a flat or find something.'

It didn't work out like that. I was trying to retake my maths and media studies GCSEs at Hammersmith College and, as Mum had pointed out, I only had my one-day-a-week wage from Saxone to spend. Renting an ordinary flat wasn't possible. I burst into tears one night when Dennis asked me more about what had happened with Mum. Once the floodgates were open I couldn't stop. I told him about the rows and about Mum's constant accusations. He knew how much I loved her, but I told him that I just couldn't take it any more. I said that Mum made me terrified of the whole world. 'She says Dad is evil, but he's not. He's the only person I've got left,' I said. 'I don't know where he is, but I know I can find him. I can get out of your way and live with him.'

Dennis sighed. He was happy for me to stay as long as I wanted. But I didn't feel I could. So the next day I went to see Nico in Dalston and got the full story on how hostels worked. She told me who I should contact to get emergency housing. First of all, I spoke to the people at Alone in London, a charity that helps vulnerable and homeless young people in the city. I went to their drop-in centre in Euston to fill in the forms and explain my story. They told me that whether I would be able to find housing depended on need and availability, but in my case they were pretty hopeful. I was too. Just talking to people about my problems helped me feel I could deal with them. I knew I was walking in the right direction. I wish all kids knew that there are people who can help if you're in a bad situation.

I was referred to a hostel in Kilburn and allocated a room. It was an ordinary, pretty smart residential building on Callcott Road, just off Willesden Lane in Kilburn, north-west London. My room had a decent bed, some built-in cupboards and a lock on the door, and it was clean. Better still, I had friends in the room below. Vickie, a girl who'd gone to my old school, was living in the hostel with her sister. How amazing is that? As we caught up and gossiped that first day, I relaxed completely. I was buzzing with confidence. Vickie warned me about some of the other girls in the hostel, but I didn't really listen. It was a nice, safe place. How bad could these other girls be?

I found out at night, when the mayhem began. The double room next to mine was allocated to a refugee from Somalia. She was never alone. At least three women lived there full time and at weekends there could be ten, twelve or maybe more – in the room, on our hallway, even sleeping on the floor of our bathroom. All of which was against the hostel rules. None of them seemed to speak more than a few words of English, usually in an aggressive tone. I don't know why, but there was hate, pure hate, in so many eyes when they looked at me, perhaps because they saw me as the blonde, British girl who wore sexy clothes and make-up. As the days passed, I got so angry about being judged. Was it me who left used condoms on the bathroom floor every night? Was it me who had sex in the hallway while all the others looked on?

Every night, I locked the door and pulled the bed over against it as well, just to make sure I was safe. No matter how desperate I got, I was too afraid to get up for a wee in the middle of the night. I didn't want to interrupt what might be going on outside. This was supposed to be a refuge, a safe haven, but most of the time I was terrified. I knew that downstairs Vickie and her sister were shitting it every night too, but at least they had each other. Had my mum been right? Maybe the world was a frightening place. Maybe it was right to hide yourself away.

After less than a week in the hostel, I went back to Mum's to get some things and try to speak to her. I wanted to explain why I had left and I was desperately hoping she would ask me to move back in – anything to get away from the girl gang in the hostel. But Mum was out and she'd changed the locks. That hurt me more than anything. I felt like I'd taken a blow. It was like being beaten up again. I stood in the communal hallway with my useless, out-of-date key and I cried. I couldn't believe that she'd already taken the trouble to get someone round and have me locked out of our house. I could hardly ignore the message there. She really didn't want to see me again. Dad was long gone; Mum had given up on me. I walked away from Albany Street in shock and in tears. I had to make a go of life in Kilburn.

I got a lifeline after my first crap month at the hostel. Out of nowhere, my old friend Jessie got in touch. She'd left home and needed somewhere to stay. I needed support and felt so much stronger when she moved into my room. Jessie also gave me the confidence to fight back against the bullies next door, though it was one of the toughest battles I'd fought.

I started it by knocking on my neighbour's door. It was a weekday morning, when the place seemed as quiet as it ever got. She answered and I tried to talk to her and her friends. When I realised how little they understood me, I tried to make gestures to show that it was wrong for all the crowds to be in our hall, for all the sex and the noise to go on. Then I smiled, said thank you and trusted them to be decent people. How stupid was I?

Two, maybe three hours later, the hostel was alive with all the usual noise and mayhem as the hangers-on came back. There were more fights than ever. For the next few nights, Jessie and I hid away in my room and tried to drown out the noise from next door with our music. There was nothing Vickie, Jessie or I could do, and it seemed wrong to us to be living like this. This wasn't how anyone was supposed to live. It was doubly wrong for people who needed to rebuild their lives in safety.

The next day, two of the girls came into the kitchen while I was by myself and started on me, calling me a 'fucking bitch', for no apparent reason. They so clearly wanted to frighten me enough to get me to move out.

There was a part-time warden living in the street who watched over our hostel and a boys' hostel nearby. Finally, I decided to go and see her to complain. I said I was prepared to argue my case in front of the other girls. I said they were bullies, violent and intimidating. I guess you could say I grassed. But I did it for the right reasons, plus I had no one else to turn to. It turned out that the management were already a long way down the line towards evicting the girls. My complaint was the final nail in the coffin. They were out by the end of the week.

But there was bad news to come. My part of the game wasn't over. When I returned from college with Jessie the day after the girls had gone, five of them were waiting for us at the end of Callcott Road. My heart was thumping. I knew well enough that they weren't going to turn out to be softies like the boys from the Haggerston Estate. So did we walk on or run? Looking back, I think I was still pretty naive at that point in my life, but somehow I knew that in my new world everything was based on saving face. Show weakness and you're lost. Show you're scared and you will be. Because they'll go for you and enjoy it. So Jessie and I walked on. We didn't even cross the street. Then, when we got alongside the girls, they jumped me.

The first of them pushed me sideways, the second punched me clean in the face, the third pushed me down and the fourth kicked me. Down on the pavement, I knew what this was about: I was taking all the kicks because it was me who had complained about them. Jessie was screaming, fighting, desperately trying to get help and pull the bitches off me, but they didn't want to hit or kick her as much as me. They just swatted at her because she was pissing them off and making their job a little harder. Their job was to make me bleed and show me who was boss. It was revenge. A vicious, sharp pack attack. They had a point to prove. When they reckoned they were done, the kicking stopped. They shouted stuff in Somalian, laughed and disappeared.

'What are we going to do, Ash? We can't stay here now,' said Jessie when we were back in the hostel trying to clean ourselves up. 'That was just the first time. They'll be back for more. They'll kill you next time.' But I knew they wouldn't do it again. I had lived this weird, sheltered life, but somehow I had the ability to read people. Maybe it was because of my mum's insistence that everything happens for a reason and everything has its place, but somehow I knew I'd been jumped because I'd stood up to the girls. I also knew it was over. They would never hurt me again. And if I needed to take a beating for a peaceful life, then so be it!

Life in the hostel was quiet for a while, and Jessie and I were getting on brilliantly, though I think my being a vegetarian was a bit of a nightmare for her. Her family ate meat at every meal and after a couple of weeks of my food she decided she was going to fade away and die. 'I'm going to make myself a real spaghetti bolognese,' she said one day and headed out to the corner shop. Trouble was, the only meat it sold was frozen beefburgers. Jessie got them, cooked them and crumbled them up over her spaghetti. It must have tasted as bad as it looked, because she pretty much decided she might as well stick with me and stay veggie.

Our new neighbour was a girl called Melissa. She was there because her mum had got into drugs and then started using their flat as a brothel for herself and other women. It grounded me to get a reminder that, for all my mum's craziness, I'd not suffered as badly as some.

I was determined now to aim for a better future. I'd been struggling with my GCSE retakes at Hammersmith College and decided I would be better off doing something more practical. I found a hair and beauty course in Hendon and got a grant from the Prince's Trust to help me get the kit I needed. I won't lie, I did spend just a bit of that cash on myself as well. At least I did get a BTEC in the end, though, so the charity got a return on its money. And I had a great laugh getting qualified.

One of my best friends at Hendon was a black girl called Kisha. We always paired up to practise on each other. It didn't always go well – at least not for me. Take the day we were doing eyelashes. Mine were blonde, so Kisha got ready to dye them blue-black. Then, because my eyebrows were blonde, she decided she should do those as well. 'No way, Kisha, you've got to leave them alone,' I said.

'It's OK, babe, trust me. I'm not touching them. I'm just putting this on them for a second or two. It'll just cool them. It's not a dye,' she lied. I felt some cold wet liquid on my forehead. Then she disappeared. I couldn't open my eyes because there were chemicals in the lotion that would sting like a bitch if I did. 'Sorry about that, babes, I had to go to the loo. I'll just clean all this off now,' Kisha said when she came back.

Then she said the two words no beautician should ever say to a client at the end of a treatment: 'Oh, fuck.'

'What the fuck have you done?'

'Nothing, babes, it's nothing.'

'Get me a mirror!'

We couldn't find one, but I soon had a pretty good idea of what I looked like. Everyone who walked past our little cubicle stopped open-mouthed. 'Well, that looks . . . nice,' one of them said. I think a different four-letter word would have been more appropriate. I nearly fainted when I finally went next door to the hairdressing area and saw myself. I had the biggest, blackest most hideous eyebrows in the world. I looked like Bert from *Sesame Street*. Kisha panicked. 'It's all right, babe, I've got this,' she said, grabbing some bleach from the hair class. We went back to our little cubicle and she smeared it on my face. 'Oh, fuck,' she said again. My eyebrows had gone green. I nearly started to cry. 'It's OK, babe, I'll pluck them.'

So she did. She plucked away until there was just one little line of green hair left. My eyebrows had gone from perfectly normal to massive and jet-black to green to plucked within an inch of their existence in a single afternoon. They stayed super-thin and green for nearly a month. Thank God for eyebrow pencils.

I headed home from college one day to find that Melissa had been badly beaten up by a girl called Barbara. She'd lost a tooth, had a huge gash on her cheek and was well on the way to having two big black eyes. There were big red slashes of colour on our hall walls. When I walked in, I wasn't sure if it was lipstick or blood.

'Why did she do it, Mel? What was it about?' I asked. But Melissa wasn't telling the whole story. She tried to say that Barbara was worse off than her, that she gave as good as she got. It was all about saving face and misplaced honour; silly and sad, as I think back now. We could never admit that we were just scared little girls with no one to save us.

Barbara wasn't satisfied with just one fight. I never found out where she lived, but she hung out around Callcott Road terrorising our hostel all the time. I was her next target. I can't lie, I was petrified of her. I lived in total and absolute fear of her. I'd tried to be strong up till then. I'd tried to believe I could stand up to people. But when it came to Barbara I lost every bit of confidence and I stopped believing that I could make wrong things right.

Her first attack on me happened just around the corner on Kilburn High Road. She grabbed me from behind. I never even saw her coming. 'You know what I'm going to do to you? I'm going to slash your fucking face open. I'm going to cut you from one side of your face to the other. You're going to have scars so deep no one will ever look at you again, you fucking bitch. You think you can get away from me? Don't pretend you're stupid or I will fuck you up.' Then she let me go, pushed me to the ground and disappeared. I remember just looking after her, more shocked than scared. All I wanted to do was ask her why, and why me.

She kept the threats coming. She backed them up with real violence. She never let up, so you could never relax. One time, I got back to the hostel and she was in our shared kitchen. The door to my part of the communal cupboard was open. It was all so silly and trivial, but my cereal boxes had been slashed open, my tea and coffee emptied on to the floor.

'What are you doing?' I asked. 'That stuff's mine.'

'Fuck off.'

'You're going to have to replace that.'

Maybe I hadn't lost my spirit altogether, or maybe I was just being more stupid than ever. The food never got replaced. I'm embarrassed to say it was me who had to clean up the kitchen once Barbara left. Still it went on: threats from a girl I barely knew and who I'd never once crossed.

Maybe a week later I was in tears in the kitchen. I'd left my laundry in the drier. Barbara had somehow got into the hostel, taken the stuff out, slashed through every piece of clothing with a knife and left a note that read 'Next time this is what I'm going to do to your face, bitch' on top of the pile. I cried in my room, desperate not to be seen or heard. If Barbara came back in, she mustn't know that she was winning.

I know now that I was living in quicksand up in Kilburn. The more bad things there were around me, the easier it was for me to sink to new lows. Somehow I seemed to attract violence. At that year's Notting Hill Carnival, I'd been dancing around and having a laugh with my mates from the hostel when someone had grabbed me from behind. I froze in shock. It was the girl who'd attacked me with the snooker balls at West Acton Tube station. She'd found me. I didn't have time to speak, even if I'd known what to say. The girl just grabbed the bottle of cheap champagne I had in my hand and poured it over my head. Then she threw the empty bottle back at me and disappeared into the crowds. If I'd been feeling insecure before, then it was ten times worse afterwards. I started to look over my shoulder everywhere

I went. I never felt safe. I let myself slip. I began to do things that would have made my mum cry. Stealing was first, though I swear I only did it because I was cold. It was freezing in the hostel that first winter and I hadn't taken a warm coat with me when I left Albany Street. I went down to Oxford Street in my thin summer coat and got tempted. I found a great fake-fur number with a hood and just walked out of the changing rooms and then out of the shop with it on my back. No one even turned a hair.

After that, I was just a little bit hooked. My mates thought I was mental and I embarked on a sort of nicking spree for a phase. It all stopped when I was leaving a branch of Accessorize and noticed a tall, handsome store detective. He was listening into his walkie-talkie. I could hear that the person on the other end was describing me. I stood there, frozen like a rabbit in the headlights. Suddenly, this didn't seem like a bit of fun any more. The detective turned and looked right at me. Then, as my life flashed before my eyes, he did something weird and wonderful: he winked, nodded me away, and turned ever so slightly aside to let me escape. I didn't need to be offered a second chance; I legged it. I didn't nick anything ever again. Well, except for food.

Sometimes Melissa and I had no money and were starving, so when we went to the supermarket we'd eat while we walked – eating cheese or whatever and hiding the empty wrappers behind things on the shelves.

'Where did you have dinner?' people would ask us.

'Sainsbury's!' we'd say.

Other times, we'd put a JD Sports bag in the near end of the trolley. Then we'd walk the aisles, making a big display of looking closely at things. All the budget stuff – spaghetti and sauces and cereal – got put in the front of the trolley. Anything costing more than a pound or so was accidentally dropped into the JD Sports bag. We'd get home giggling like, well, girls. 'Look at the food we've got!' We were so ingenious about our cooking. We deserved to win *Masterchef* for managing to make something out of nothing every day. Forget Jamie Oliver and his food for a fiver; we could cook a meal for 50p or less.

Something wonderful happened one night when we were making one of our super-cheap feasts. We realised that Barbara had disappeared. She'd just stopped coming round. For a few weeks, I acted like my mum when she'd been trying to avoid Dad. I was terrified and looked over my shoulder every time I went out or downstairs into the kitchen. But as the weeks went by, I got to relax. Barbara had been a bizarre nightmare and now she must be haunting someone else, I decided. That turned out to be just as well, because Melissa, Jessie, Vickie and I were about to need all our energy for a new set of battles. Some of the Harrow Road Boys had found us. It was all going to get very ugly.

CHAPTER NINE

●

BAD BOYS

'd never even heard of the Harrow Road Boys till I moved to Callcott Road. I'd never heard of the NW Massive or any of the other gangs who patrolled their different patches of turf in north-west London. I didn't know that postcodes mattered or that invisible boundaries shouldn't be crossed. I didn't know about the war between north and east London boys.

One of the guys had chatted Melissa up when she was out and after that they started coming round to the hostel that winter. The first time, there were about six or seven of them, some white, some black, some mixed race. Most looked about 19, but strip away the swagger and I reckon some could have been younger. One of them, though, was in control.

'Who is he?' I whispered at Melissa.

'I'll tell you later,' she whispered back.

Later happened when the main boy and his crew decided they wanted a Chinese takeaway. They also decided that Melissa and I would go and get it for them.

I was so pleased to be getting some decent food for a change. We'd never had such a big order from the Chinese before. We got all my favourites. It was great. What soon became clear, though, was that after the boys had been around once – and once we'd fetched their food – they would be around all the time.

There were about six or eight of them in the core gang, but there were many, many more on the edges. The hostel became their cotch; when they wanted a refuge from the police, their homes or just their everyday lives, they came to our refuge. They turned it upside down.

Were they laying down some sort of marker that first night we went to get them the Chinese? If they wanted us to know we'd never relax again, then it was mission accomplished, because we walked back into a knife fight. When we got back with the food one of them was up against the other, knife against his throat, threats pouring out of his mouth.

'What took you so long?' asked someone. That was what stunned me the most. While two of the guys looked set to kill each other in one corner of our tiny room, the others just wanted to eat their takeaway. They made violence normal. The boy who'd had the knife at his throat disappeared the moment the other one let him go. No one said a single word as the guy with the knife joined us at the table. Threatening to slash someone's throat didn't even justify a comment. The scar on the knife guy's face told me he would probably have carried out his threat if the food hadn't arrived and if he could have been bothered. It ran right across his left cheek, down a high, taut cheekbone, through the corner of his mouth and down to his chin. He'd been knifed himself, so why wouldn't he knife someone else? Why would he need anything more than some stupid reason to do it?

I watched his every move as he ate, worried that he might kick off again at any moment. I was petrified. This was everything my mum had been trying to protect me from. I couldn't believe how quickly this had become my world.

It was freaky how often violence kept breaking through into our lives. It was always there when the boys came round. It would be swirling under the surface, exploding in some stupid act of aggression when one of them thought someone had made him look like a fool. The wrong word, the wrong glance, a crappy joke: it could all kick something off. I first saw a mass brawl in the late summer when one of the guys pretended to drop someone's gold chops chain down a drain. They all came rolling back into our hostel, and the guy who thought he'd been dissed was letting his rage build up. All he'd suffered was a stupid playground joke, but he couldn't take it. None of them could take that kind of joke. He lashed out in our kitchen when we tried to calm him down. Then he got jumped and they all joined in. There was hardly any room to fight inside and when some of them tried to get away it spilled out into the street. There were no knives that time, just punches and kicks and blood. After a brawl like that, they'd all be back a day or so later, honour intact, tight as a family, playing best mates against the world again.

They intruded so much on our lives. There was one time when I was in Melissa's room watching TV with her. One of the boys came in, unplugged it, picked it up and walked away with it. 'We're watching that,' I said, but he was a big guy and we just let him go. I'm almost as ashamed of that as of anything else I've ever done.

'You can't fight them, Ash,' the other girls said, but I thought maybe I could, especially as I'd just found my first proper boyfriend. He made me feel strong. I thought that we could take on the whole world together. Stupid girl. My dreams didn't last for long. What a disaster my little love affair turned out to be.

I'd sort of wooed him with a Walnut Whip. He'd been selling T-shirts outside Wembley, where Jessie and I had gone to see a Jodeci concert. We'd dressed ourselves up and blagged our way to the front because we wanted to get close to DeVante, who pissed everyone off when he didn't show up. A bit of fun and flirting with the guy on the merchandise stall afterwards made me feel better. His name was Daniel, he lived in north-west London and had a full-time job. Amazingly, I'd actually walked past his work and clocked him back when I was living with my uncle Dennis. Now we finally got to swap numbers. He called straight away and I thought I had it made. What I liked most was that Daniel was working. He didn't just waste his days like all the boys in our hostel. He had a future and was going somewhere. That had to make him one of the good guys, right?

I went to the dole office near his work every week to sign on to get my rent paid. I was still only working part time in the shoe shop while I finished college. Seeing Daniel after leaving that place always felt great. There was an undercurrent of violence there almost as strong as at the hostel. I could never believe how many people threatened self-harm, or worse, if they didn't get their payments. I don't know how the staff did their jobs.

Anyway, I handed over the Walnut Whip the first time we met for a drink. I don't know why that seemed like the last word in romance, but it did. Things started well enough. After hanging out a bit, we even decided to have a weekend away – down to Margate in Kent. It wasn't exactly Miami or the South of France but we had a good time. We stayed in a hotel and we were like an old married couple. We sat in a pub, had fish and chips, went for walks. I liked it all.

What I didn't like, though, was how everything about Daniel could change in a heartbeat. I couldn't believe I'd managed to find a volatile, unpredictable man. As if we didn't have enough of those cotching in the hostel without me bringing back another. At first, I brushed away my worries because Daniel was good to me. He helped organise me and looked after me. He reminded me that having a job and earning a wage was normal and that made me ambitious again. Daniel also reminded me of my mum. While she was obsessed with her religious stuff, his thing was conspiracy theories. He'd talk about things like faked moon landings, where Aids had come from, wars, what the Government was doing, all that sort of stuff. He actually made me want to read, learn and stretch my mind, which hadn't happened for quite a while. However, like my mum, he could be very full-on, and he got intense about our relationship very quickly. He also got weird.

I was playing cards in Melissa's room one night when he came over with some flowers he'd bought me. The trouble was I never got them. One of the Harrow boys had grabbed them off him, ripped them up and stuffed them in the bin down in the kitchen. He'd also told Daniel that I didn't really like him and that he liked me now so Daniel should basically piss off. It was a schoolboy taunt, really, but unfortunately it hit home. We had a bit of a row and Daniel stormed off, or so I thought. An hour or so later, I went to the loo and heard some noises. At first, there was just a rustle. I was terrified of rats, so that in itself was enough to freak me out. Then there was a sort of cough. The sounds were coming from the airing cupboard. I swung open the door and there he was. Daniel, a full-grown man, hunched up in a cupboard and sitting on a boiling hot pipe.

'What the hell are you doing there? You scared the life out of me.'

'I'm hiding.'

'Why? From what?'

'So I can watch you. I want to check you're not cheating on me.'

Cheating on him in our communal bathroom? That should have been all the warning I needed that the boy wasn't quite as stable as I'd thought. It should probably have told me that the relationship wouldn't end well. But it didn't. All my life I'd known people who weren't 'normal', so although it was weird, it was what it was, if you get me.

I should probably have dumped him the day we had a fight on the roof of my building. We scuffled and I fell off but, by some miracle, just managed to grab the edge of the roof at the last split second. I was hanging on to the concrete edge for dear life. Daniel grabbed at my arms. He was crying and trying to pull me back up, but I was too heavy for him. I knew I couldn't hold on for much longer. I started to slip; I was losing my grip. Daniel held on to my arms even tighter. I thought I was a goner. I was crying. I begged Daniel to let me go because he was starting to slip himself and I could see that if he didn't let go of my arms, he was going to fall with me. It felt like a film; everything seemed to be happening in slow motion. I closed my eyes and begged God to save me.

At that very second, one of my toes touched a window ledge below. I told Daniel to let me go. At first, he wouldn't because he thought I'd fall. I told him he had to and it would be all right if he released me slowly. He eased me down until both feet were on the window ledge. It was so narrow that I had to put my feet sideways. Then, using one hand on the underside of the window frame to brace myself, I used my free hand to knock on the window, attracting the attention of the Chinese tenants in the top flat. Thank fuck they were at home! I was saved, just as I had been at the Tube station in Acton. Daniel held me tight and said how sorry he was, how scared he'd been. I gave him a second chance because he promised me that everything would be calmer from then on. It wasn't.

The rows went on; the ups and downs got even more dramatic. So I made my move one night after we'd been to the cinema. He was walking me back towards the Tube. 'Daniel, I need to talk to you,' I began. 'I'm trying to sort my life out. I want to finish college and get a job, and I think I need to be on my own for a while to do it.'

He was very quiet, but his eyes were alive. 'I can help you sort things out.'

'I know you can. But I want to do this on my own. I want to prove that I can.'

There was another long pause.

'Is everything cool?' I asked.

'Sure. It's OK. You go,' he said.

I gave a huge sigh of relief. I don't think I'd realised how nervous I was until that moment. I'd been so worried he would fly off the handle that I hadn't even considered he might take the news well. 'I'll see you onto the Tube,' he said. A true gentleman.

'No hard feelings. I'm going to get my life together. Then maybe we can see each other again,' I said as the southbound Northern Line train pulled into the station.

'No hard feelings,' he said as he climbed into the empty carriage after me. Then he punched me in the face.

'What are you –' I could only force out three shocked words. He punched me again. I tasted blood. He hit me a third time. I was scrambling on the floor of the carriage, terrified and in total shock. He stood back from me and stepped away. I took my chance. I stood up and lunged for the emergency stop lever. That was the moment Daniel fell apart. I screamed for help and I think he snapped into reality and saw what he had done. 'Ash, I'm so sorry. Oh, God, I didn't mean it. Please don't tell anyone,' he said, moving towards me. But I pulled away. It was too late to keep quiet. The train driver and someone from the station were running towards us, yelling at Daniel to keep away from me.

They called an ambulance for me and the police for Daniel. He got arrested. I had to give statements and then I was told I'd have to give evidence against him in court. It was a terrible time. Daniel and his mum used to ring me day after day, begging me to stop the court case.

I had to think of his future, of his job, they told me. They said he needed professional help, not punishment. They said he hadn't meant it, it had been an accident, a one-off, he would never do anything like this again. His mum said his dad had beaten her; it was what poor Daniel was used to. I don't think I could have stopped the case even if I'd wanted to and, besides, my mum's voice was always in my head, telling me I had to make a stand. Men shouldn't hit girls; bullies shouldn't win; crimes shouldn't go unpunished. I was in between a rock and a hard place. So I met Daniel's mum halfway. I didn't go to court, and I let the police get on with it without my help. But if I thought that was the end of the violence in my life, I was mistaken. It was swirling all around me.

Three days after Daniel attacked me, I was walking down to the shops with Melissa. My face was fucked. I had two deep black eyes, a bruise down my left cheek and a cut above my eye where Daniel's ring had caught me. One of our friends, D1, passed us in a car. This guy who was with him asked me who'd beaten my face.

'Nobody,' I said. Today I'm embarrassed I replied that way. Don't women always say 'nobody' when they've been beaten up by someone they love?

'Don't look like nobody to me,' he said. 'I'll find out.'

A few days later, D1 brought the guy round to the hostel. He was one of the biggest, strongest and, yes, best-looking men I'd seen in a while. He was the biggest and strongest man I'd met since I last saw Dad. He was wearing sharp dark clothes and he looked totally in control of life. I liked that. I needed it.

'I know who hit you,' he said.

'It doesn't matter who did it. I'll get over it. I won't look like this for ever,' I said, trying to change the subject and flirt a bit, even though I must have looked like Quasimodo. He saw past the state of my face and by the time he left we'd made a connection. His name was Marc. We swapped numbers and he said he would meet me after work the next day. I'd got a new shoe-shop job, on Kilburn High Road this time. He walked me home some nights, drove me home others. We hung out for a while and I got to like him. We weren't actually dating and hadn't even kissed.

Then one night, after my shift, we were heading north towards Willesden Lane when I saw Daniel on a side street. He was wearing my hat. It might sound silly, but that stupid hat meant a lot to me. I'd saved for it and I'd forgotten that he'd borrowed it. When I told Marc, he said, 'Wait here, babe. Don't get out of the car.'

'What are you going to do?'

Marc was already walking away. He was heading towards Daniel. 'I just want to ask him why he hits girls,' he shouted back at me. His voice scared me.

'Is your name Daniel?'

'No. Who's asking?'

'Is your name Daniel?'

'No.'

'Well, I think it is. So do you enjoy hitting girls in the face?'

Daniel tried to lie his way out of it, but Marc wasn't having a bar of it; he took a swing. His fist connected with Daniel's face, just where he had hit me. Daniel crumpled. 'What the fuck are you doing?'

Daniel's mate made a stand. 'That's enough!' he yelled.

But Marc wasn't finished. 'You want some too?' he asked as the guy moved in to protect his friend. 'Do you think it's right what he's done to Aisleyne's face?'

Daniel's mate said nothing.

'Come on, babe. We're done. No one's going to hit you again,' Marc said, wrapping his huge arm around me as he got back into the car. I leaned in against him, too shocked to speak but strangely happy. I hate violence in any form, but it made sense in our world back then.

In one way, everything about what I had just seen went against everything I had ever been taught. All of Mum's religions, all her lessons had preached that violence was never the answer. But in another way, it seemed the right thing to have done. Wasn't this just the modern version of an eye for an eye? Didn't everyone have the right to hit out and avenge injustice? If so, then Marc was on the right side of the line. Then there was something else. I didn't feel on my own in those first few moments after the attack; I felt as if this big strong man was looking after me. Mum had often said that my dad could have looked after us. On her good days, she made out he was a hero. That was the kind of man I'd wanted all my life.

Marc asked me out a week later. I knew my mum wouldn't have liked what Marc did to Daniel but I told myself that Mum would approve of Marc's character – his belief that a man should never hit a woman. That was what Mum had taught me. So I closed my eyes to all the grey areas in Marc's life. I was 17, he was 27 and I wanted to be loved. I focused on the fact that he had defended me. We started dating and I relaxed with him totally. I began to rely totally on him. I completely forgot I was supposed to be sorting my life out on my own. I was happy and I felt safe.

'It didn't matter if I ever dated you or not. I had to get justice for you.' When weeks later we talked about what he had done to Daniel, that was what Marc said. That was how it worked in his world. That was the code of honour all the boys lived by.

Things had changed for me from the first moment word got around that Marc had lashed out on my behalf. They changed even more when people realised we were a couple. It was like *The Sopranos*. I couldn't add it all up at first because, apart from that one fight, Marc was such a gentle, decent guy. He was kind to me and he seemed one of the most stable people I'd ever met.

Marc had a friend called Mark Lambie. The two of them had serious reputations, which at first I was oblivious to. (As it turned out, Mark Lambie's reputation was justified. Over the years, he became a major north London gangster.) I remember one of the Harrow Road Boys slapping my arse as I walked up the hostel stairs; before I had a chance to mouth off, his mate had already pulled him up on it, saying, 'You can't do that, she's Marc's girl.' It was like living inside a protective ring of steel. Any threats that came my way bounced off the two Marks' reputations. Being bullied at school, beaten up on West Acton Tube station, terrorised by Barbara and others at the hostel, attacked by Daniel – it was all just a memory now I had Marc on my side. Suddenly, I got respect. It felt great.

Marc lived in a hostel as well, over in Harlesden. He and I did nice things together. We'd go to the cinema. He had a blue Jag and a black Golf and we'd go for drives like a pair of pensioners. Late at night, we'd go to Aries, the 24-hour booze shop on Willesden Lane, and buy Jamaican patties and Cherry B, a naff drink you got in miniature bottles and which really appealed to my sweet tooth. Marc would help me out, buying food when I couldn't afford any. I was intimidated by restaurants back then. I'd been brought up eating dinner off my lap, so I couldn't handle how formal they were. I felt uncomfortable sitting facing someone while all the staff watched everything you did. We would eat at a really relaxed pub up in West Hampstead, or we'd just have a takeaway, rent videos and hang out. Marc treated women well. He always opened doors for me and made sure I got into his car first. There was something lovely and old-fashioned about him. He was a perfectionist and I liked it. With him, I had a wonderful feeling of everything being safe and easy. I felt I could coast through life with Marc. No one got in my way and for the first time in a long while I didn't need to look over my shoulder as I walked down the street. It was time to live. I was ready to party.

Just before my 18th birthday, on 28 December 1996, I got a cheque for a couple of grand, compensation from the Criminal Injuries Board for the Tube station attack on my way back from school all those years ago. I decided to blow it all on the best party ever. I rented a massive sound system, got the drinks in and begged favours of MCs and DJs to pull it all together. I had IC3, a big jungle MC, to take control. A whole group of new friends who I'd met through Melissa were coming over from the World's End Estate, the place where my mum and dad had met. It made me feel good to have links to the place where it had all begun. When the big night came, the whole hostel was packed. We'd even got a few guys to work the doors as our security. The music blew the street away. Marc brought a magnum of champagne. I didn't know bottles came that big. Over the rest of the night, I did my best to drain it. Maybe that was why I didn't notice the change in atmosphere until it was too late.

Everything was cool when Marc was in the hostel. It always was when he was around. Everyone was on their best behaviour in front of him. But just before midnight he said he had to go. He hated being around when any of the Harrow Road Boys were with us. Plus he was just about stealing my thunder; everyone wanted to talk to him, as if he was a celebrity. He hated the hassle of that. And on my birthday, it all fell apart when he had gone.

Some guys from south London arrived. Since the Harrow Road Boys were there too, even I knew this was not going to be good news. A couple of fights broke out in the street and then it kicked off inside as well. One guy was rowing with Melissa in the kitchen and I saw him holding a can of CS gas in her face. I must have thought I was Superwoman but I was right there between them.

'Stop it, calm down, it's my fucking party.'

'Get out of the way, Aisleyne.'

'No, I won't. Get out of my party.'

I grabbed the gas canister and tried to force the guy to put it down. Why exactly I thought I might be strong enough, I don't know. He told me to get out of the way again. 'Your friend is too cheeky, Ash. I'm sorry but it has to be done,' he said. Then he reached his arm around me and gassed her in the face. 'She shouldn't run up her mouth,' he said. Then, for some stupid reason, he took our toaster and our kettle, I suppose because they were the nearest things he could see, before he and his mates legged it.

'They wouldn't have done that if I'd been there,' Marc said when I told him about it the next day. 'Do you want me to get the stuff back for you, darling?' I thought again of the times Mum had said Dad could have protected us if he'd been there. I realised how life could be if a strong man loved you.

For the next few weeks, I was blissfully happy with Marc. I started to dream about a long-term future at his side. We used to talk about a house, kids, the lot, sometimes in jest and sometimes for real. Then, suddenly, he went missing.

I only had his mum's house number and his pager number. Normally, I'd get a call within minutes of paging him. But not long after my birthday everything went quiet for days and then weeks. I didn't think he had just been using me. I was more insecure than most, but I was still pretty confident that we had a better connection than that. So where the hell was he?

The hostel buzzer went just before midnight one night, just when I was really starting to go spare. 'Darling, it's Marc.'

'Where the hell have you been?'

'I'm sorry, darling.'

'What the hell are you doing?' He was undoing the belt on his jeans and pulling open the buttons. In our hall, after being away without a word for nearly three weeks. 'As if, mate,' I started to say, but then I saw why he was doing it. 'Marc, what happened to you?'

He had a knife wound all the way down his left leg. It had 30, maybe 40 stitches running through it.

'Come upstairs,' I said. 'You've got to tell me what's been going on.'

He sat on my bed and told his tale. A little 14-year-old boy. The younger brother of one of his mates. A boy being bullied by some Yardie man. 'It wasn't right. I had to help him,' he said. But when Marc went to be a hero for this boy, just as he had been for me, the Yardie and his mates had a machete. The guy had tried to chop his leg off. He'd needed an air ambulance to get him to hospital and he'd been kept in for nearly a week. We lay back on my bed. I think I was just so happy to have this big, strong man back in my life that I closed my mind to the way all this violence had become normal. It was the world my mum had changed everything to protect me from. Now it was all around me and I didn't even question a thing.

We settled back into a nice little routine. While I started to open up and tell Marc about my family and my past, I did keep a few secrets from him. The biggest was what I looked like without my make-up. I got away with it because of the way we lived. Every time we met followed the same pattern. I'd page him, he'd call me back, we'd make an arrangement, then if he was coming over, he would call again just before he got to the hostel. That was my ten-minute warning. I'd run to finish off my hair and put on my full make-up. When he stayed over, I'd sneak out of bed at 6 a.m. so I could look perfect for him when he woke. What a saddo!

He thought it was hilarious. One time he told Melissa he wanted to know what I looked like without my make-up. 'I'm serious,' he told her. 'You've got to help me so I can see.' So he called her one time and she let him into the hostel without letting me know. 'Hi, babes!' he called out. 'It's me. Let me get a good look at you.'

I screamed louder than I'd ever screamed before. This felt like the lowest blow in the world. I ran upstairs to try and hide; I curled up on the floor, my head in my hands, grabbing at a nearby coat, desperate to cover myself up. 'Don't look at me! Don't look at me! I'm butters! You'll never fancy me again!' He grabbed me, trying to uncurl me and see my face. I screamed even more. He tickled me and kissed me and finally got me to put the coat down and stand up. I was out of breath and red in the face, a total, unmade-up mess.

'Happy now?' I asked.

Funnily enough, he was. 'You're beautiful, darling,' he told me.

He still wanted to see me. But I was about to see a little less of him. Because I'd just had a call from my dad.

CHAPTER TEN

●

HAPPY FAMILIES?

We had a payphone on the ground floor of the hostel, next to the room of a new girl from Jamaica. In six months, I don't think she got a single call herself, but she still happily answered all of ours. Bless her, she even took messages.

'A woman for you Ash-a-leen,' she called up to me one day. I could barely be bothered to head downstairs. If it wasn't Marc, I wasn't interested.

'Hello. Who is it?'

'Ash, babe, it's Nico's mum, Eilish. I can't talk long, but you're going to get a call in a couple of minutes.'

'Who from?'

'I can't tell you.'

'You've got to tell me.'

'Well, it's your dad. He's gonna answer all your prayers. He's minted and he's going to make it all OK for you. Good luck, Ash.'

The line went dead. I paced jerkily up and down our tiny little hall, never letting myself get more than an arm's length from the phone. I stared at it, willing it to ring. I tried to stop my breathing sounding like I'd just done a marathon. It rang.

'Hello?' It was Dad's deep Barry White sort of voice. I'd forgotten how much I loved it.

'Hello.'

'Is that you, Aisleyne? Do you know who this is?'

'Yes.'

'Who is it, then?'

'It's my dad.'

There was a long pause. On the other end of the line it sounded as if he had run a marathon too. 'I can't believe you're calling me your dad. Thank you, darling.'

And so it began. We talked for five, maybe ten minutes, saying nothing at all, really. Then I made the move. 'Can you come over and see me?'

'If you want me to come, I can be there on Friday.'

It turned out he already knew where I was living because he'd hired a private detective to find me. One week earlier, my friend Chanelle and I had come back from a club in the early hours. It had been snowing and we'd danced around in the street like kids. Then, when we were nearly home, Chanelle had written our names on the windscreen of a car. She misspelled my name. Amazingly, Dad walked by that night. We must have missed each other by seconds. He saw it and corrected the spelling. By the next day, it had all melted away so I never saw that someone had fixed my name.

'Come on Friday. Come whenever you want,' I told him. When the day came, I was in a panic. If I needed to look good for Marc, then I needed to look fantastic for my dad. I screamed the hostel down. I wanted everyone to help me, advise me, lend me their best stuff. And everyone was there at my side when Dad arrived. Everyone wanted to see the man I talked about more than any other. He didn't disappoint.

Dad rocked up in a sleek white Porsche with red alloys. That's the big white horse of the modern day, right? I was a princess. He was the king, the hero ready to sweep me off into a better world. I could hear my mum's voice ringing in my ears as Dad parked the car: 'Don't be impressed by worldly possessions.' I could remember the teaching from all the different religions that said the same. But I was impressed. In fact, I was ecstatic.

'Your dad looks like a copper, Ash,' one of the boys whispered. He did. He was clean-shaven. He was wearing a nice shirt and jacket,

Versace jeans, good shoes. When he got closer, I could smell great aftershave. He had a bit of a belly, but he looked fit – big and strong. He was just the way I wanted my dad to be.

'These are for you, Ash. I know you like 'em. They remind me of your beautiful, happy, smiling face when you was a little girl.' He was holding a massive bouquet of sunflowers. 'I got you 18, because I missed your 18th.'

That was when I started to cry. All the others faded away a bit, and Dad and I ended up in the kitchen on our own. I put the sunflowers in the sink while I nervously fussed around filling up a vase.

'Come 'ere, princess,' he said. We hugged so tightly. All the missing years faded away. Suddenly, I knew that Dad wouldn't ever let go of me again. I felt as safe in his arms as I did in Marc's. All I ever wanted was to feel safe. Now I did.

'I've missed you, Dad. I love you. I wish you hadn't gone away.'

It was Dad's turn to cry. My big, bad dad. Here he was, in tears in my arms in the kitchen of a crappy little north London hostel. In that moment, I was in heaven. I forgot all the bad stuff dragging me down. I forgot all the things that had gone wrong. This was my dad, my hero. He was finally back in my life. All the prayers I'd said since I was a little girl were going to come true. He was going to make everything better. Maybe, just maybe, he could help me with Mum too. I felt sure that all my worries were over. Nothing this good had ever happened before.

When we stopped crying, we didn't stop talking. It felt easy, that first time. I told Dad about the people in the hostel, about how I'd lost my way but I was going to find it again. Just talking to Dad brought my dreams into focus. I heard myself say I wanted to go back to college full time. I heard myself say that I wanted to go up a gear from selling shoes in a high-street branch to being a buyer for the whole chain. I heard myself say I would leave the hostel and get a proper flat somewhere safe. I liked the confident, focused girl I was imagining. I promised myself that I would live up to it all. I had someone to do it for now; I felt I could be ambitious without being embarrassed about it.

'You're making me so proud, princess,' he said. 'We mustn't lose each other again.' I said we wouldn't. I told him I loved him. More tears. He said he'd thought it would take me ages to be able to love him again. I couldn't understand why he'd think that. I loved him instantly. I'd always loved him. That was why he'd never been out of my mind. That was why I'd always been looking for him.

He was a regular visitor from then on, always in the Porsche but never flash with his cash. The second time he came round, he brought me a KFC. (I had started to eat meat because I was so insecure about being too skinny and thought a bit of chicken breast might give me some breasts of my own!) The third time, he took me to Chicken Cottage on Cricklewood Broadway. We kept things light by hardly ever talking about the past and never talking about Mum. He took me round to my nan and grandad's house in Southgate, then on to see my aunt Sue, who lived just around the corner. My four little cousins were there as well. It was the first time I had seen any of them in so many years. It was all very weird and very emotional, meeting your relatives while feeling like a stranger. Nan's house was just lovely and ordinary and safe. They still had their TV in a cabinet. Grandad still played golf in the hall. Auntie Sue's house was just as normal. I was so happy just to be there.

'Can I take the kids out to the park?' On that first visit, I was so determined to be the perfect older cousin. But when we're playing a game on the swings, my cousin Kiera only goes and breaks her leg. I was totally mortified. I was convinced they would blame me and never let me see the kids again. Instead, they forgave me. Or at least they did as soon as poor little Kiera stopped walking with a limp!

Back in Kilburn, the happier Dad and I got, the more enemies we made. I can see why the other girls might have been jealous that I'd been saved, but I hated how they acted. Melissa was the worst. One day, Dad and I were chilling in my bedroom, watching TV together, when Melissa started ranting and raving about her passport. It had gone missing and she was asking again and again if I had it. Basically, she was just mouthing off so she could show off in front of my dad. Then she made it worse by saying something bad about me. I don't remember exactly what it was, but I know she totally disrespected me in front of this man I had just rediscovered, the man she knew meant everything to me.

The Aisleyne my mum had brought up wouldn't have cared. She had been taught to turn the other cheek. But the Aisleyne who lived in a hostel was different. I'd started to think a different way there. Respect and honour mattered to me, even if they were ridiculous and unearned. I am mortified at what happened next. I lashed out at Melissa. I knocked her drink out of her hand and I lunged at her belly to throw her off my bed and out of my room. We both wrestled and went for it on the bedroom floor – pulling hair, screaming, swearing, the lot. Dad leapt in to pull us apart. I was ashamed and embarrassed about the whole thing. I didn't want Dad to think I was violent, but then I didn't want him to see me lose face. I didn't want him to feel he had to look after me, but I wouldn't have wanted him to look the other way while I got beaten up either. That whole incident left me totally confused.

Dad made a decision, though. 'Princess, you've got to get out of here,' were his last words when I took him downstairs to say goodbye that night. 'Aisleyne, you can move in with me,' were his first words the next time he came round. They were pretty much the best words I'd ever heard. I was going to live with my dad. I was getting out of the hostel. I was finally going to be like everyone else.

Dad had a modern, ordinary council flat on the Regent's Park Estate in Camden. It was less than five minutes' walk from Mum's place. So for all those years we had been living right up against each other. When Mum had gone on about seeing him walking or driving past our windows, she'd probably been right. I could have found him years earlier. Maybe everything would have been different if I had.

But no regrets, right? I threw myself into my new life with Dad. I loved his world. The flat had a big telly, leather sofas and a bedroom for me, and I absolutely adored it. I felt comfortable there from the start. And I was so proud of my dad. He was really into cars, and we talked about that a lot. It turned out he'd actually raced cars professionally in the past. He'd had sponsorship and everything. I wished I'd been around him back then. When I was a girl, I'd always pictured Dad as successful and glamorous like that.

The only bad thing about it was having to share Dad's place with his girlfriend. Petra was too skinny and too nervy for me. The first time I met her, I couldn't get over the fact that she had no boobs. I mean, I was no Pammy, but I was still growing. She was wearing a suede dress and she had a great tan, top blonde hair and some classy gold jewellery. She looked rich. But she didn't work and I didn't like that. The way I saw it, she just ponced off my dad. We circled each other in the flat and in Dad's life like two wary cats, our insecurities flaring up in lots of bitchy little rows.

I never got to the bottom of what Dad did for a living. What is it with men and their secrets? I think his job really did have something to do with second-hand motors. 'I'm a car dealer, darling,' he said once, giving me a big wink to suggest that at least part of that description was true. He was really proud of his car-racing days and said he'd made a lot of money off sponsorship. Whatever the truth was, he always had plenty of spare cash. I was scared to rock the boat by asking too many questions. I didn't want to lose him by looking uncool or turning back into some kind of goody two shoes.

'This is my dad,' were my new favourite words. I loved bumping into people I knew so I could introduce them. Playing happy families was everything I had hoped it would be, and for a while it just kept getting better. Dad, Petra, me and some of the others in my new-found family went on a couple of holidays together. This was the life I had always wanted. Just walking through the airport with them all made me feel good. I was finally doing the kind of thing that normal, average families do. We holidayed in style, as well. The first trip was to Spain, where Dad rented a private villa and an open-topped 4x4. Then we went to Gambia and I slept in a vast room on stilts over the ocean.

'Here's £100 – go get yourself some bikinis,' Dad had said to me just before that trip. I was as excited as a schoolgirl. I rang one of my girlfriends with the news. 'I've got a hundred quid!' I screeched. We went shopping and I spent every penny in that shop where the store detective had let me leg it. I thought I owed him that.

Gambia was amazing, but the memory of it is tarnished by one incident. I sat on some of Petra's clothes in her room and she screamed at me, 'Get off my clothes! Who do you think you are, the Queen of fucking Sheba?' I wasn't losing face in front of Dad, so I went for her. It took Dad and his African mate to pull me off her. Bloody pride – it's a comfort to fools only. Remember that, kids!

• • •

Dad and his girlfriend were in the kitchen; I was in the bedroom with Nico and a couple of boys. We were talking and joking, chilling in for the night. But then a bell rang in my mind. The television was on mute in the corner of the room and as I looked at it, the local news for London began. 'I have to watch this,' I said, though I never usually watched the news. 'Where's the remote?'

I upped the volume, which pissed everyone off. Then the story began. There had been a drive-by shooting in Kensal Rise. Suddenly, I felt certain of something: 'It's someone I know,' I said in a whisper.

It was. It was Marc.

The news hadn't actually named him. While his pager took my message, he didn't return my call. Within minutes, one of his mates rang. He told me what had gone on. The shock was like a blow to the head. It was the sock of snooker balls all over again. But this time the hurt didn't fade. It still hasn't. To this day, when I think of Marc, it feels like it did the first day I got the news. It feels like boiling needles are being fired into my skin, and into my heart.

Marc only just survived. He was in a coma for what felt like for ever. I tracked down his mother, who I'd never met before, a dear and lovely old Jamaican lady in Harlesden. The first time I spoke to her on the phone, I could tell that something in her had died, as had something in me. She was a sad, proud woman. She didn't deserve this pain. For the whole of that first year, I wrote Marc letters. Some were just silly little notes; some were massive, five or six pages of my thoughts. I didn't know if he would ever get to read them. Then, one day, the clouds parted. His mum gave me the news when I called: the doctors had seen good signs. They said he looked ready to come round, and they were right.

We talked on the phone for months and months before he would let me visit and see him. The first time we spoke, I asked him, 'What happened, Marc?' All along, I'd wanted to hear the story from him.

'I was just hanging out,' he began. His voice was all raspy and tired. He said he'd been at his hostel as normal when Mark Lambie had come round. 'Let's go food shop,' Mark had said. My Marc had gone, even though, he said, he hadn't wanted to.

'I didn't wear my chain,' he told me. It was gold, from India, and had a diamond-studded panther hanging from it. I'd touched that chain round his neck so many times when we'd been dating. I'd even worn it sometimes myself. It was Marc's talisman. 'Is that why they got me?' he wondered. 'Because I left it at home?'

What had happened had been a screech of brakes outside the shop while the two Marks and a few others lined up to pay. The place had been sprayed with bullets. One guy got killed, right in front of his little son. My Marc took a bullet in the neck. Mark Lambie walked away without a scratch. He was the one they'd been aiming at.

Marc coming out of his coma was the biggest rush of my life. But, as with so many of the highs in my mum's life, it was followed by a low. Maybe everyone's life is like that. The doctors felt that regaining consciousness was the best Marc could hope for. They said he should stabilise after that but that he would never really get any better. He was paralysed from the neck down. This strong, passionate man would stay like that for the rest of his life. He knew it. I wasn't surprised that he didn't want me to come round and see him.

Trying to shake him out of his depression by phone was so hard. The more Marc withdrew, the more I loved him. I realised that whenever I'd looked ahead in my life, I'd included him in my dreams. Not so long ago, we'd been laughing and joking about having children. His rich, gorgeous dark skin, my light hair and blue eyes – they'll be stunners, we joked. Now we would never know.

Marc kept talking about the machete wound to his leg. Was it his destiny to be paralysed? Had he been so bad that this was his punishment? We'd always talked so much about karma and cause and effect. Well, if this was cause and effect, then karma had royally fucked up. My Marc was a hero, not a baddie.

When I wasn't on the phone to Marc from Dad's, I was trying to open my eyes to what was going on around me. I needed to wise up to some of the things my mum had grasped all those years ago. First was the realisation that Dad wasn't necessarily the best person to anchor your life around. Our lovely flat turned out to be an illegal sublet. Dad had paid some mate for the key, but after the first six months he pretty much stopped paying the rent. It was time to go. But Dad had a plan.

'I've already got you a better place,' he told Petra and me as we were packing our things together. Our new home was up in Southgate, behind electric gates. It was part of a private development and felt as cool as anything. Our neighbours were rich people, young professionals, hard-working City types. I don't think they knew what had hit them when we moved in.

My mission was still to work out what was going on with my dad and drugs. Was he using? What and when? All I had were questions. I was forever looking for clues. It was the not knowing that did my head in. I can cope with the truth, try to find solutions to things, but I hate being left in the dark. How can you move forward if people aren't honest with you? So I noticed every dodgy smell, every odd noise. I worried every time Dad had a lie-in. I was a paranoid wreck. I checked out all my dad's visitors. I questioned everything. I just needed to know the score – quite literally!

Bit by bit, I worked things out, though I still tried to think the best of everyone. When Dad had special lights set up in the bathroom so he could grow weed, I still told myself that was small stuff and didn't matter. Nor did I worry the time I discovered a suitcase of cash. It just seemed like the plot of a film. It was under Dad's bed and I found it when I was looking for a bag to take some junk to a storeroom. I'm not going to lie: for a split second I considered running away with the money and starting again. I was tired of all my paranoid thoughts and constant questioning. But I couldn't bring myself to do it. Instead, I rang Chanelle.

'What are you going to do, babes?' she asked.

'Nothing. What can I do?'

'You could take some of the cash. He owes you.'

'No, he doesn't. He's my dad. I love him and he loves me. He's letting me live here, man. Nah, I can't . . . can I?'

'Well, take some for me,' she joked. 'Or at least get enough to buy yourself some new clothes.'

In the end, I took three twenty-pound notes – sixty pounds from a case that must have contained tens of thousands. I still felt like a naughty little girl. I'd never make a career as a bank robber. I bought a pair of trainers with the cash, but I never really enjoyed wearing them. I felt that they'd been bought with dirty money. I've always felt torn and confused about all the different teachings of my mum's old religions, but the one message I've taken from all of them is about karma. Stolen cash, from a very dodgy source, had to be a bad vibe. I felt there was enough bad karma swirling around me already, so in the end, when Chanelle borrowed the shoes one time, I never asked for them back.

Marc was telling me that I should go out and live my life, so, little by little, I got back into partying. Going to clubs and dancing took my mind off everything that was going on at home. I drank a lot of champagne. I decided that was the image to aim for: the blonde bird who only drank the most expensive drink in the bar. It got me noticed, and I started making some surprising friends.

The most bizarre was Barbara. Yes, the girl who had terrorised and terrified me back at the old hostel. I saw her in a club in Camden and felt an immediate jolt of the old fear. When she headed across the club towards me, I was absolutely petrified. But instead of attacking me, she apologised to me. It had been just like Smelly Kelly at school, although on a bigger scale. Barbara had bullied me to impress the people who were scaring her. She'd been trying to climb up the psycho social ladder and prove how hard she was. In that club in Camden, it was pretty clear that she wasn't so tough after all. It was dark and noisy, but she looked and sounded like shit. Her life had hit a truly bad patch. Medical problems, bad sex, drugs: everything had been whirling around her and dragging her down. We talked a lot that night and afterwards. We never quite got to be bezzy mates, but we came to an understanding. Life's amazing when you think about it, and people are surprising. Not every enemy stays one for ever.

A place I loved to go back then was Parkers Bar in Finsbury Park. We would all go, a big gang of girls, passing a bottle of vodka around the top deck of the 29 bus and loosening up for some really fun nights. On one trip, we got the whole of the top deck singing songs from *Annie*. How funny is that? It was the best bus journey ever. Parkers was right in the middle of an area with a big Turkish population. All the men seemed to love us blonde girls and I just loved being the centre of attention. One of my friends, Destiny, was a dancer at the club and, seeing how much fun she had, I tried to get a job alongside her. She was so much more talented than me and had some great routines. I just tried to wing it alongside her. In the end, I landed a job behind the bar. The going rate was £5 an hour, but I got a little extra because I worked it so much more than the other girls. I somehow got a whole new crowd of locals coming into the bar. I adored the job. I'd spend forever getting dressed up and ready. I loved the feeling of putting on a show. I even had my picture taken for a Turkish-language newspaper when they did a huge piece about the club's bright new bar girl. At least, that's what I hope the piece was about!

I started dating again at Parkers. The guy who'd done the dance auditions reminded me of Marc. He was a real entrepreneur, which I liked. He owned a radio station as well as a whole load of bars and clubs. More importantly to me, he looked and acted similar to Marc. He had the same hands. When we were together, I felt as if I was still with Marc. By the time that little scene ended, I was ready for something more serious. I convinced myself I'd learned enough about men to tell the good guys from the bad. Then I went and picked the wrong ones all over again.

CHAPTER ELEVEN

I'M SINKING

A tall, strong man called Shaun was the first hottie to catch my eye. He had really lovely parents who had a big old house in Finsbury Park. I was envious of how close he was to his family. He did a bit of acting, which was exciting. He was also a brilliant cook. I'd watch him make three-course meals for a dozen people and think it was the best skill in the world. We dated for a while and had one wonderful holiday together. He booked a trip to Florida, ten blissful days in the sun – ten days that would come back to haunt me when it turned out that they were paid for on a stolen credit card.

Then there was a sportsman called Darren. He had the most amazing hazel-green eyes, plus a great body, so no surprise that all the girls fancied him. When we first met, he looked like he might really be going places. He picked me over all the hot girls who were after him, and I adored him. He treated me so well (like the bad boys always did), but there were always shadows in his world. 'Ash, don't stress. It's not crack. It's not as bad as you think,' he lied when I first got on his case about drugs. He would smoke in his room and come out with his green eyes blazing.

After a few months of my nagging, he realised he couldn't deny what he was doing, so his story changed. 'It's cool, babe, it's nothing to stress about. I only do it on weekends.' Then it was only on

Mondays or Wednesdays or Fridays and so on all down the track. 'Relax, babes. Just chill. Try some.' He passed me the crack. That was me in the danger zone. Somehow I got through it. I got passed those smokes so many times. I came so close to taking them, but I never did. My boyfriend was slowly letting himself be controlled by the 'white witch'; I couldn't lose control along with him. If he was going down, I needed to be able to look after him. Besides, something inside told me I could be an independent woman like my mum. I didn't want anything dragging me down. Plus, I knew I had no one to catch me if I fell. So I kept on saying no.

In the clubs, I didn't stick to my old deal of just drinking champagne. I wanted more fun and I went with the crowd, taking a lot of Es and basically getting fucked up. Back at people's homes, there was even more going on. I went round to Barbara's for an after-party one night and realised her friends were very heavy people. I ended up lying on the floor next to some overpowering Yardie guy. He passed me something – I don't know what it was but I think it was crack mixed with LSD – and that time I wasn't strong enough to pass it on. He was too close to me, too insistent, too full-on.

The next thing I knew, I was in Barbara's kitchen and this guy was all over me – hands, tongue, everything was everywhere. I couldn't stop him. My mind was playing tricks on me and I almost felt obligated to let him do what he wanted. What the hell had I taken? Fortunately, just as the guy was about to do some real damage, he suddenly just lost it. He let go of me, turned away and stumbled back into the darkness of the living room.

But I was still wrecked. 'Barbara, I've got to get home. You have to get me home,' I said, again and again. She got me there, but the trip was only just beginning. On my bed, I was hallucinating and hearing voices. 'This is very, very bad,' my own voice was telling me, like some sort of freaky schoolteacher. Then I felt a weight, as if some huge man was on my chest pushing all the air out of my lungs. I closed my eyes for a moment and then I was too petrified to open them again. What if there really was some man on top of me? Could the Yardie guy be back? Had he followed me and got into my room? Next, I started to hear voices shouting my name and the sound of people storming up the stairs. They were coming to get me, but I didn't know who they were or why. I could feel tears pouring out of my eyes and running down my cheeks, but I couldn't move any part of my face. I realised I couldn't make any expression at all, nor could I move a single muscle in my body. Somehow, I was looking down and seeing a black-and-white picture of myself. I was all serene and still on the surface, but I was losing some terrible battle inside.

Then my mobile flashed and rang. Finally, I could move. It was like I'd had a near-death experience and Nokia was the light at the end of the tunnel. It was a mate called Winnie. He was my saviour, telling me to turn away from the darkness. 'I need you, Winnie,' I told him, delirious, 'and I need Tissam. She's my sister. I need to be safe.'

'I'll come get you, Ash,' he said. But when he came round, he'd decided I was ready for even more fun. I got into the back seat of his car, where a gang of girls was laughing and shrieking. I had sunglasses on so I could look a bit more normal and a bit glamorous, but I was crying like a baby. My make-up was a mess and I had tears running down my face. 'Where are we going, babe?' I kept asking from the zoo in the back seat. 'Are you taking me to see Tissam?' He was, though only after dropping everyone else at some after-party at a club and trying to persuade me to follow them in.

Tissam was an old friend from my first secondary school. She lived with her parents on the Lisson Green Estate, north of Marylebone, and her flat was dangerously high up. 'I need to fly,' I kept saying to her while she tried to calm me down. 'I need to jump off your balcony so I can fly.' She laughed and locked all the doors and windows. That night, she held me close in her bed for hours. I always felt safer in someone's arms.

A week later, I was at Darren's and I had a terrible vision of his future, maybe of mine as well. He was on his way to losing everything: his looks, his money, his talent and his potential. Would he lose his life as well? I wanted to fight to stop it. 'Babes, let's go out. Let's have some fun today.' I tried so hard to get him out of his flat. He'd captivated me at the start with his energy and the air of excitement around him. He was a sportsman, a tough guy, an action hero. But everything was changing. As the months passed, he did less and less.

Sitting in with him, trying to pretend I was pleased to see the stream of druggy visitors, I felt our world get ever smaller. We lived in London. The whole world was out there on our doorstep. But we never left our postcode. I was worried out of my mind because I knew we were throwing our lives away.

Going home to my dad's didn't help. The atmosphere was pretty bad there, too. Dad was getting the same kind of visitors as Darren. His mood swings were getting out of control. There'd be stupid arguments and sudden rages. I'd wanted so much to be happy there, but I started to get scared instead. I felt like a fog was creeping over me some days. Everyone else's bad stuff was seeping into my life. It really hurt me to know I couldn't fix things for the people I loved.

The only way I could shake off the gloom was to close my eyes to it, so I went into denial overdrive. I convinced myself that Dad couldn't be doing serious drugs. I think I genuinely got myself to believe that his problems had to be something else, that they had to be something out of his control. I thought of the lady with Tourette's syndrome and the guy with the leather trousers at the Jehovah's Witness meetings. I remembered the way the brain tumour had affected my other uncle's mind. I thought back on all the people I'd known over the years who had had problems with mental health. Dad had to be the same, I told myself. While that wasn't good, it meant he could get cured.

It was Marc who put me straight. He'd come out of the hospital and social services had found him a flat in Harlesden. He was my first port of call for advice when life went wrong, even though we still only spoke on the phone, as he didn't want me to see him paralysed and weak. I would ring him in the early hours to tell him about my dad's mood swings and pass on my latest theories about schizophrenia or some other mental illness. 'Ash, wake up. You know that's not what's going on, darling,' he kept telling me. 'Are his hands swollen? What about his ankles? Does he eat lots of sugary things? Is he still sleeping all day? Ash, you've got to admit he's on something.' No, he wasn't. Not my dad. 'Do you want me to speak to him for you?' Marc asked at last. That one got me crying. There was Marc, paralysed but still my hero, still wanting to sort things out for me. I said I would deal with it on my own.

Dad and I had a family day out planned. Petra was away, my aunt Sue was coming round and he was going to drive us to a big car-boot sale out in South Woodford. After that, we'd probably grab something to eat and chill. I had an intense fear of speaking out to my dad. I didn't want to break up the life we had found, having already lost him once. But I knew I had to say something, and I felt our day out would be the perfect opportunity to really talk. So, although I was scared, I prepared myself. I needed to hear the truth. I rehearsed all my arguments, made little lists of all the things I wanted to say and convinced myself that I could make everything OK. Then the big day arrived.

Dad hadn't surfaced when I went for a shower that morning. I banged on his door on the way to the bathroom. 'Wake up! We need to be ready to go in half an hour.' Nothing. I had my shower, got dressed, did my hair and make-up, and looked at my watch. No sign of Dad. Auntie Sue arrived and I could see her outside in the car, talking on her phone. I headed for Dad's door. 'Get up! We're waiting for you. I'm coming in.'

I nearly got thrown off my feet by the stench in his room. It was so strong you could practically see it. Smell is one of the things they don't tell you about drugs. But I had to breathe through it. Dad was unconscious on the bed. The sheets were littered with his junk: the foil, the spoons, the crap. 'Wake up! Dad, what's the matter with you? Wake up!' Nothing.

I pulled open the window, threw water on Dad's face and began slapping his cheeks and shaking his whole body. I'd never felt so alone. When he came round, I ran out to Auntie Sue. Don't ask me why, but I felt humiliated, totally ashamed, to have to tell her what had happened. This was the moment I had to come clean about what my dad was doing. It was real, it was happening and I had the proof. I felt as if it was my fault that Dad had lied to me and betrayed me over what he was doing. It all hit me in the face like a brick. It took my breath away. I was on a rollercoaster rushing downward, speeding into a black abyss, and there was no way to stop it and get off.

The rest of the day was a total blur. Later, just at the time I'd thought we'd be having a nice afternoon walk out in east London, we tried to talk about what was going on. Sue had called my nan and everyone had come over to try and deal with the situation. Dad wasn't exactly happy, and he blamed me for telling everyone. It was the ugliest afternoon. 'We just want to help you,' his mum said at one point. He said he didn't need help. I know now that you can't save someone unless they're ready to be saved. It went on and on. All the time, I was trying to be the peacemaker, but I kept getting flashbacks to that time so many years ago when he'd slit his wrists in the bathroom. I loved him and I was so scared of losing him, but I couldn't stay in his house now that I knew the truth about what he was doing.

So when our sad little family conference was over, I packed my bags and went back to my nan's house. Life with Dad was over. Everything seemed frozen in time. I lay on the sofa in Nan's living room. The street lights from outside created a beautiful orange glow on her ceiling. For some reason, I couldn't even cry. What took my breath away was how stupid I'd been. Why had I believed in Dad for so long? I'd had him on a pedestal all my life. I'd refused to accept any of the bad things Mum said about him. I hadn't even let myself see what Marc had seen. Somehow, I had to get over it and move on.

• • •

'Mum, it's me, Aisleyne.'

There was a long, awful silence on the line.

'Are you there, Mum?'

'How did you get this number?'

I couldn't believe she said that. It was the old number. She hadn't changed it. Years ago, it had been my number too.

'Please, Mum. I really need to talk to you.'

It was the day after I'd left my dad's flat and I was at my nan's. I'd not spoken to Mum in nearly three years, but that day I just had to. I opened the floodgates. I told her about the fights with the girls in the hostel, about the boys who'd terrified me, about what had happened to Marc and about finding Dad unconscious the previous day. When I finished, there was another cold silence. 'Are you still there Mum?'

'Of course I'm here. What do you want from me, Aisleyne?'

'I don't know, Mum. I just wanted to talk to you. Can I see you?'

'There's no point. All of this is what happens when you go away from God. That's what I taught you and what I tried to tell you all your life. You brought it all upon yourself, Aisleyne. Now I really don't know what you expect me to do. You can't expect anyone to help you now.'

'But, Mum . . .'

'Aisleyne, you've brought all this upon yourself.'

I kept on trying to get through to her and she kept pushing me back. She said I should have known my life would end up this way. One thing came over loud and clear: my problems were all my fault. She couldn't help me. The conversation was over.

I didn't move for a long time after she hung up. So many memories were running through my mind. I could see my mum in the good times. I remembered how much fun she'd been and how much she'd wanted to protect me. How could someone so good choose to turn her back? I needed her so much that day, but I knew I'd lost her. So I had to pick things up on my own. 'Don't cry, Ash,' I told myself. Then I rang up the same agencies that had found me the room at the hostel last time around. I told them about my dad, about Marc, my mum and all the issues that were building up and the things that were going wrong around me. 'Would you have somewhere I could live?' I asked, mortified that my life had taken a step backwards.

They called me in for an interview and we went through all my options. I felt as guilty as hell. The adviser said that when someone moved out of a hostel once, it wasn't usual for them to come back again a second time. They said they wanted hostels to be stepping stones to a better life, not fall-back places people could dip in and out of whenever things didn't work out. I felt awful. 'I understand that,' was all I could say. 'I'm so sorry to be back here asking again.' The adviser and I didn't speak again while we both finished off our bits of paperwork. Then he gave me my second chance. He found me a new address and I promised never to screw up again.

CHAPTER TWELVE

SECOND CHANCES

I was thrilled, excited and full of energy when I moved out of my nan's. I'd had to spend a few extra weeks on her floor when some administrative hitches pushed me back down the hostel waiting lists. But the agencies were just terrific. They don't just talk about where you're going to live, they talk about courses, colleges, training programmes, all the things you can use to lift yourself back off the floor. They kept me informed, made me feel optimistic and assured me that everything was going to be OK. They were right.

The place they found me was wonderful. I had a room in a hostel on Bayham Street, right in the heart of Camden. There were only three rooms. I was nearly 20 by this time and the other girls were slightly older than the ones who'd been staying in the Kilburn hostel, too. While everyone had problems, there was an edge of ambition rather than violence in the air. It lifted me up. I was still working in the shoe shop and behind the bar in Finsbury Park, so I had a bit more cash coming in. I talked to the store manager in Kilburn about the company structure and how I could get that buyer's role in head office.

One of my new neighbours in the hostel was a cool hippy girl called Sophie. It felt like good karma that she was a sort of young version of my mum. She had a similar name and the same passion in life. Sophie was a dead-keen fashion student and we talked for hours about clothes and design, as well as different courses and colleges. Something was calling me to follow her into that world, if only to try to make my mum proud of me at last.

My friend Tissam was always around too. We had such a laugh together. In my first week in Camden, there was a huge rainstorm and for some bizarre reason we grabbed some shampoo and ran outside to wash our hair in the street. The neighbours must have thought we were mental.

In the hostel, all the girls and our visitors were cool. We all cooked together, did our hair and make-up together, swapped clothes like sisters and just got on like a house on fire. For the first time in my life, I finally felt like a carefree teenager. I loved the feeling of living without fear and having so many bezzy mates. Through Tissam, I made loads of other friends in the area as well. One of them was Joe Cole – we hung around with the same people just before he hit the big time with West Ham. I heard a shout of 'Hey, Aisleyne!' one day from a guy in a yellow Mercedes. I didn't know anyone with a car like that. It must be another Aisleyne, I was thinking. But it was Joe, in his first flash car. I was so happy for him that day.

Not long after I moved, someone else called out to me in the street. I was heading up Bayham Street early one evening when someone shouted after me, 'Aisleyne – is that you?' It was one of Mum's old Jehovah's Witness friends. The Kingdom Hall we used to go to in Pratt Street was just around the corner. I couldn't remember the woman's name, but I recognised her straight away.

'I can't believe you remember me,' I said, feeling all teenage and self-conscious again.

'Aisleyne, we talk about you a lot. Why don't you come and join us for a coffee after one of the meetings?'

I'm so glad I did. They were still good people. They didn't judge me; they greeted me as an old friend. They didn't make me feel as if my life had gone off the rails and they didn't say bad things about me letting go of their faith. They sympathised about what had happened with my mum.

Spending a bit of time with the Witnesses again grounded me. Having the odd cup of tea with them in a Camden café was just lovely. And I was already feeling good. I'd had a brief wobble when I'd moved into the hostel because I'd felt I was taking a step backwards. In the early hours, I would lie awake worrying that I was treading water and not learning from any of my mistakes. But I snapped out of it. With a new friend like Sophie and a whole group of old friends from Tissam to the Witnesses on my side, I felt ready for anything. It turned out I needed to be. Marc was finally ready to see me.

At his flat, he had full-time carers who looked after him in shifts. The main one was a lovely lady called Elizabeth. She was there my first visit. She saw me cry as I left. My strongest memory of that first trip to see him is of holding his hand for the longest time. If you'd asked me when we were going out what part of his body I liked the most, I'd have said it was his hands. They were so big, so strong and they held mine so well. Once, I'd drawn an outline of them on a sheet of paper. Now I couldn't bear to look at the drawing. No physiotherapist can really do much for your hands when they're paralysed, so they wither away. They become old man's hands, ghostly hands. Just one physical proof of all the pain.

Over the next weeks and months, I saw a lot of Marc and his carers. They were all just brilliant. They had to do the lot, helping him wash and go to the toilet as well as feeding him. Marc was a perfectionist, though, so sometimes I would go over the washing up or hoovering just so he was satisfied it was done how he liked it. Marc had some great kit so he could at least try and have a more normal life. Voice-activated phones and computers helped. For a long time, Marc vowed that all of this would help him live his life again. For a long time, he coped.

The first promise he made to me was that he would carry on being my hero. He would keep my protective shield intact. He got a mate to buy me a car so I could visit him more often. I still kept praying for a miracle. I prayed that one day my old Marc would be back and we could start again where we'd left off. In the meantime, I kept writing him silly little poems. I'd loved writing poetry as a kid. Now I started again, jotting things down and trying to put all my feelings into words. Most of the time, I was too embarrassed to read them out loud. Instead, I kept them in a little box I bought specially for the purpose. I'll read them out to Marc when my prayers are answered and he gets better, I thought. Then we'd laugh about what a big softie I'd become.

Leaving Marc's flat and heading back to the hostel was never a good journey. I always got the shivers when I went anywhere near the scene of the shooting in Kensal Rise, so I used to drive as far around that part of town as possible. Bad memories cast such long shadows. To this day, I still feel uncomfortable there and try to avoid the area whenever I can.

It was always a relief to get home. The hostel was a really nicely done-up three-bedroom flat. We didn't have a living room, but we had a huge kitchen. And, best of all, it was calm. With just the three of us – me, Sophie and an Eritrean girl called Etaya – getting on with our lives, there were no hangers-on, no gangs, no condoms on the hall floor. I turned into a right little queen bee, drawing up cleaning rotas and firing out house rules so we kept it all nice. I was determined to keep the routines going as the girls left and got replaced by new flatmates. I think I actually enjoyed the challenge of training new residents into my ways. The girl who replaced Etaya was pretty much the only one who really fought against me. She was a posh girl called Jennie and she didn't like being told what to do. I think she was used to ruling her own little roost and we sparked off from the start. I wasn't thrilled by the fact that she told me she was only in our flat so she could live for free while she saved up to buy her own place. She had a good job and made tea in a glass teapot, for God's sake. Maybe there was more to it than I knew, but was she really in need?

I never once doubted that I had been right to move out of Dad's flat, but I got confirmation pretty quickly. A whole load of clothes and stuff – including my childhood photos, all my photos of Marc and some of the poems I'd written for him – had gone into storage when we'd moved to Southgate. But when I went to collect my things and take them to the hostel, I found out that Dad had only paid one month's rent on the unit. 'All that stuff was sold or dumped months ago, love,' the woman on the desk told me. I think she thought I was crazy, because, instead of blowing up and throwing a fit, I just started to laugh. I laughed like a mad woman. Wasn't that just so bloody typical of my dad? Taking a good first step, letting us all think everything was OK and then screwing up. On the way home, I tried to make a mental list of all the things I'd had in those black bin-liners. Who might have bought them? The woman at the desk had looked pretty much my size. Had she been given first choice? I should have taken a closer look at what she'd been wearing. Now I thought about it, her skirt had looked a bit familiar. So there I was, back to square one, starting from nothing again.

Despite that setback, I felt optimistic. I didn't have a full-time job because I was planning on going back to college, but I had got back in touch with Aunt Ingrid, who had moved to a flat in the Barbican, and she paid me to do her ironing once a week. I also did some voluntary work at Play Space on Ladbroke Grove, where we looked after disabled kids and gave their parents a break for a while. That felt good. I'd walk home from those shifts convinced that if my mum's old theories about karma were right, then I could finally expect things to get better for me.

When, six weeks after moving into the hostel, someone from the housing association came round for one of their regular visits, I was just fizzing with optimism about the future. 'Is it all working out for you, Aisleyne?' he asked.

'It couldn't be better,' I said. 'I've never been this happy living anywhere in my life.'

'Well, it's one of the best hostels we've got. We're relying on you girls to keep it that way,' he said.

I waved him off that afternoon just full of pride and self-belief. I felt like the good girl I'd been brought up to be. It was lovely to be recognised for doing something right for a change, and I was totally determined to repay that man's faith.

It wasn't to be. Less than two weeks later, we were raided by the gun police. The whole street was cordoned off while they turned our rooms upside down. Some of the neighbours were kept out of their homes for the night. The police had had a tip-off.

CHAPTER THIRTEEN

●

POLICE RAIDS

'Ash, it's Sophie. You need to get back here. The police are raiding us. They're looking for guns.'

My heart almost stopped. It was the early evening and I was on my way back from a day out in town.

'I don't understand –' I began.

Sophie interrupted. 'Well, they're in your room, Ash.'

I couldn't have got back to the hostel faster if I'd flown. All the way, my heart was hard with fear. I knew I didn't have a gun. I'd never even seen one. But I'd learned a few things back in Kilburn. One of the biggest lessons of all was that a bad man doesn't keep a gun in his own house. He keeps it in some stupid girl's house instead. That way, she's guilty, even if she's innocent. My mind was racing. Who could have done this to me? It must be someone from back in the Kilburn days. How had I become that stupid, stupid girl?

'You need to let me through. I live in there. I think they're searching my room.' They held up the police tape and I got escorted inside the hostel. It was full of police, black uniforms, silver flashes and hi-vis jackets everywhere as they moved like ants over every inch of our home.

'You're Aisleyne Horgan-Wallace?' A plain-clothes guy took control. He looked a bit like my dad. They questioned me for so long.

I don't think I was supposed to see the officer giving his boss a tiny shake of the head, but I read the message. My room, the whole flat, was clean. But it wasn't over. The questions kept on coming. Who did I know? What did I know? One of the boys that used to cotch in the last hostel had told me that if you get arrested you can get off a charge if you name others who've done worse than you. Had someone named me? What did anyone think little old me could have done?

As usual, one of the first people I turned to when the nightmare was over was Marc. I was at his flat an hour after the last of the police had left Bayham Street. 'You were so lucky, Ash,' he said. 'You know someone was shot in the Camden Palace last night. That's the gun they were looking for. If you'd been in the room when they turned up they'd have had you down on the floor with a gun in your back. They'd have dragged you out of there by your hair. You need to be careful, Ash. You're not safe in that place any more. I want you to move out of there. You know you can always come and stay here with me.' He was so kind, so caring, so decent. 'I need you to need me, Ash. I need to be your hero again,' he said then. Tears started to fall out of those big, lovely dark eyes. Tears he was unable to wipe away. But he was my hero, paralysed or not. He was my best friend and my confidant, my strength. I just wish I'd told him that then, not waited until it was too late.

I never got an answer or found out the truth behind the raid on the flat, but it was all I needed to send me off the rails again. Everything and everyone that was important was last on my list, and I didn't see Marc for about a month after that.

'Marc, are you OK?' When I saw him again, I got a shock just looking at his face. He'd lost so much more weight. I'd not thought he could possibly lose any more.

'I'm fine, baby,' he said. 'I'm fine now that you're back.' While I was fussing around trying to persuade him to eat, he said, 'You know we could still have those kids, Ash. It's just the process we'd need some help with.'

'The process?' How unromantic is that? I remember I laughed, but only just. 'I'll think about it. But I'm a good girl, remember. You'd have to marry me first.'

'I'd love that, babes. I'd marry you tomorrow if you'd have me. And you know you'd make a great mum.'

When I saw Marc again the following week, he was even thinner. His rich black skin was discoloured in places. I thought I was being stupid, but I felt worried that he had poisons under his skin.

'Is he OK?' I asked his carer, having excused myself and told Marc I was going to the loo.

'He's going through a bad patch. It's normal for someone in his position,' she said. 'Just at the moment, he doesn't feel like making any effort. He's decided he doesn't like me washing him any more, and he's got a few bedsores because he's stopped letting the therapists exercise or move him. He can't feel them, but they're not good and we need to keep an eye on them.'

I went back to his bedside and asked if he wanted me to wash him. He didn't. I asked him why he'd stopped eating and he just said he didn't want to get fat. Then he said something else.

'Ash, if I asked you to help me do something, then would you?'

'What is it?'

'Just tell me, Ash. Would you help?'

I took a deep breath. 'Of course I would. Anything you want.'

'I need you to help me end it.'

I remember feeling like I was a thousand miles away. Everything seemed quiet and clear and smooth. The man I loved wanted me to help him die. He was waiting for me to speak. 'Marc, I don't know what to say.'

'I've thought about it, babes. I know what I need. I know what I need you to do. It'll be quick and easy and then it'll be over.'

'Marc, you mustn't talk like this. You can get well again. We've always said you can get well. Last week, you promised to marry me and have kids with me, for God's sake. Is this your way of telling me I've been dumped?'

Marc looked away. Maybe stupid jokes weren't such a good idea after all.

'This is just a bad patch, Marc,' I said, totally serious now. 'If I speak to someone and we change your therapy or your medication, we can sort it. I know we can.'

But we couldn't. Marc carried on refusing his bed-baths and his exercises. His bedsores multiplied and got worse. Then they became infected and everything sped up. He was taken into hospital. Somehow, I'd been right in thinking he had poison in his system. He developed a severe case of septicaemia and it destroyed him fast. He had next to no fight left in him. His body and his immune system were shot, and I saw him shrink before my eyes. Day by day, visit by visit, he got smaller, older, sicker. Then it was the end.

I had half an hour alone with him on the final day. Marc's best friend Malik was with him when I arrived. I waited my turn in the hospital corridor. When Malik came out, I froze. This was one of the toughest of the tough, but tears were dripping off his face. He couldn't look at me or speak to me. So in I went to see Marc. It was terrible. His whole body was tied up to tubes, he was barely breathing and he had these plastic see-through things on his eyes. But at least I had that time alone with him. I'm so grateful I had that chance. I stroked his face, kissed his forehead, his hair and his hands. I said so many things I should have said to him before. The kind of things we never say to people until it's too late. I told him that I loved him. I said I would see him again one day very soon. It took me forever to let go of his hand when my time was up.

Marc died that evening. His family, friends and I were all camped out in the hospital waiting room. Even Mark Lambie was there. No one knew what to say or do. I went home and didn't leave my room or stop sobbing for nearly a week. Marc's family were flying his body back to Jamaica for his funeral. I wanted to pay my respects and grieve properly, but I didn't have enough money for the plane fare. Who could I ask? What could I sell? I tried to think of something, anything, as that final week flashed by, but there was no one and nothing.

'We've made all the arrangements. It's going to be beautiful. And you know Marc would have wanted you there,' his brother Martin told me on the phone. 'You are coming, aren't you?'

I just couldn't say the words: 'I don't have the money.' I couldn't bear to feel like a ponce trying to cadge some cash off them. So I made some other excuse and didn't go. God knows what the family thought of me.

Years later, I bumped into Martin and finally came clean. 'I just couldn't afford the ticket,' I said, ashamed at how pathetic my life must seem. 'I tried everything I could think of, but I just couldn't get enough money in time. I wanted to be at that funeral more than anything else in the world. I'll never regret anything more.'

Martin just stared at me. 'Ash! Oh, God, we'd have paid for you ten times over. We'd have lent you anything to be there. That's what Marc would have wanted.'

I still don't think I could have taken the loan, though. I was a 21-year-old woman. Surely I should have been able to look after myself.

Someone else died the year I lost Marc. It was Riah, a lovely lady in her 80s who I'd come to see as almost a surrogate grandmother when I was a girl. In the good times, Mum and I had eaten so many Sunday lunches at her house in Kentish Town. Riah was able to calm Mum down and bring her peace even when she was at her most troubled. One of the Witnesses saw me in the street and told me the story, which was hard to believe. Riah hadn't just died. She had died in the strangest circumstances. She'd been found with a telephone wire wound round her neck and a fork had been stabbed all over her face. Was it suicide, or even some kind of ritual murder? I never found out.

At the funeral, I saw my mum. I'd thought she might be there and I'd tried so hard to look my best in case I saw her. I'd rehearsed so many conversations, dreamed so many dreams about how we would end up in each other's arms. But the reality was different. At the funeral itself, Mum wouldn't look at me, let alone speak to me. When we all went back to Riah's family's house afterwards, she wouldn't even be in the same room as me. If I approached her, she got up and went the other way. I don't know what made me cry the most that day – having lost Riah in such an awful way or knowing I'd still lost my mum.

I carried sadness with me everywhere I went after that. It tainted everything I touched. Things were already looking bad at home. The safe, social world at Bayham Street never recovered from the gun raid. You can't just forget about that kind of menace. The neighbours looked at us differently. I'm sure they'd never been over the moon about having a hostel on their street and now their worst fears had been realised. We were clearly bad people. I felt as if I was a magnet for trouble and I began to attract even more of it.

Then one day I came home from work, put my key into my room door and the lock wouldn't turn. I asked Sophie (who'd just woken up from a nap) if the hostel agency had changed my locks. All of a sudden, I heard rustling behind the door. Realising someone was in there, I started to kick the door, trying to get it open. Then two men opened it and we all stood staring at each other for what felt like ages but was probably only two seconds. They ran past me. I had really high shoes on, but I ran after them, down the hostel stairs, up Bayham Street, through the park. I looked down and my feet were bleeding, but still I kept running. I don't know who I thought I was, but I'm sure Wonder Woman's feet ain't supposed to bleed! I gave in, crying, adrenalin pumping. I got some guy on the street to drive me around Camden in his van, but they'd vanished.

When I got back to the hostel, I inspected my room to see what had gone: my camera, my jewellery and a big bottle of D&G perfume my auntie had bought for me. I had nothing of real value, but they'd taken all I had.

Less than a month later, I was sitting in the living room of a girl I thought was a good friend when I realised that the man sitting opposite me was one of the guys who had been in my room. I was pretty sure my friend had set me up. I went down to the toilet to compose myself and saw that my magnum bottle of D&G had pride of place on the shelf! I confronted her; she denied it; he had legged it. I was devastated.

It was around this time I started to realise things seriously had to change in my life. It was hard to know where to start, though. The faces were all changing at the hostel. Jennie and Sophie moved out and I had some more hardcore flatmates for a while. They were party people, and I was glad of it. I felt I needed to have my mind taken off my worries. One night, though, I got back to the hostel and there was this guy in the bathroom. He was washing his hands and arms with battery acid. It stank and I freaked out. 'What the hell's going on?' I asked the other girls. It turned out you use battery acid to wash off gun residue. His skin went dry like a lizard's. It flaked off all round the hostel. Everyone just turned a blind eye.

We got to know some students in a few houses opposite and soon there was always some noisy get-together going on in the street. The first of my really bad nights kicked off in one of the flats next door to the hostel. A whole gang of us had been hanging out in their kitchen. Out of the corner of my eye, I spotted that everyone seemed to be ganging up on some young kid I'd not seen before. The action moved upstairs and suddenly we could tell it was serious. We could hear shouts, grunts and then screams. So up I went. The fight had begun in one of the bedrooms and by the time I got to it, there was blood everywhere. But for all the noise, there were just two people fighting, the young kid and the madman who was whacking and slashing him with a bottle.

'What are you doing? Stop it!' Here I go again with the hero act! What made me think, again, that I could intervene in a fight like that? I don't know why I always thought it was up to me to be the peacemaker. Especially when there were all these blokes just standing around stoned and letting it happen. 'I said stop!' I pushed myself between the pair of them. There was blood on me now. The bottle was very close to my face. My heart felt like it was going to stop. I was breathing as fast as the kid. I was still roaring with anger.

Somehow, I won the battle – or at least I was right there when it ended. The kid collapsed and just sank down to the ground, out cold. Then the whacked-out man just threw the bottle down onto the kid's head and walked away. He didn't even run, he just sauntered off out of the bedroom, out of the house and on down Bayham Street towards Mornington Crescent. 'Get an ambulance!' I yelled when the kid didn't come round straight away. The party was over.

I headed back to the hostel to clean myself up. An hour later, I got arrested. The police came over because one of the other girls had said I'd been the one with the bottle. She'd said the madman didn't exist. Since the kid was still unconscious, I got put in a cell – the first one I had ever seen. If my mum could have seen me, she would have died of shame. Tissam was pregnant and she was staying with me. She headed over to the police station with a big bag of Munchies and a note saying how much she loved me. She'd also written me a list of all the people she'd called to tell them about the drama. But there was nothing anyone could do to help. So I was left on my own. In the cell, there was nothing but an apology for a mattress, and the whole place stank. I was so lonely and scared. I'd ring the buzzer every half an hour just so someone would come and look at me through the little window.

'Can I just have a cup of tea?' I kept asking, like some sort of princess. When they brought it, it was cold. It all hit me as I sat on the edge of the mattress with a drink I didn't really want. I was in a cell. I was on my own. No one could fight for me. No strong man could protect me here. My breathing got fast and panicky. I was as frightened as I'd ever been. This was real and I had no way to control what happened next. So was this it for me? Could it be that no one else had seen the guy or knew who he was? I didn't understand why this girl was covering up for him and trying to blame me for what he had done. Could you really go to prison just for trying to stop someone from being killed? I started to picture myself in jail. How long would I get? Would anyone care about me, wait for me?

It was so cold in that place, but I had one new friend. There was a guy in the cell opposite. I was crying so much and I told him everything that had happened to me. 'Have this,' he said. He was only trying to pass me a bag of brown! 'If you're going down, you'll need this,' he said. Which didn't really make me feel much better, to be honest.

I don't know how close it got, but I had the very worst night before the kid finally came round. Apparently, the police questioned him when the doctors said he was well enough.

'Was it a girl who attacked you?'

'No, it was a man who attacked me. The girl tried to save me,' he told them.

I was released, but the nightmare wasn't over. I hadn't lost my ability to attract trouble. The poor neighbours in Camden were to get at least one more noisy interruption to their routines before I wised up and got on out.

The next shocker came at six one weekday morning when the drug squad forced their way into the hostel. Tissam and I woke up in a panic when the door burst open. There were three huge white men at the end of my bed. For some reason, my first thought was that maybe they were friends of my dad.

'Come on, love, you've got to get up, both of you.'

'Who are you?'

It must have been the shock, but when they said drug squad, I nearly laughed. 'It was the gun squad last time and they didn't find anything,' I wanted to say. But something told me I couldn't joke with these guys.

We got the chance to grab a few clothes – after they'd been searched. We weren't left alone for a second; they even watched when we went to the loo. Then we had to stand around while the men went through everything else we owned, and I mean absolutely everything. They went through and behind every cupboard, into the ceiling tiles, through all the clothes, into all the furniture. It was actually an incredible operation to watch. I couldn't really blame them for making sarcastic comments about our stuff. I know I'd have done the same.

They didn't find anything, of course, but that didn't mean it was over. When the search finished, question time began. Tissam and I were separated, and they were asking me about loads of the guys I'd known when I lived in the old hostel. All that seemed such a long time ago to me. 'Look,' they said wearily, 'there's no point in blanking us. We know you know these people.' Somehow, I couldn't get the message across that I hadn't really known them, even back then. I'd never known where any of those guys lived, who they really were or what they did. Most of them had gone by gang nicknames, for God's sake. How could I give any evidence if I didn't even know their real names? And why would I?

When the police finally left in the middle of that awful morning, I knew that it was all over for me in Bayham Street. I was mortified that once more a set of police cars and vans had blocked up our road and scared the neighbours. If it really was my personality that was attracting all this trouble, then it was me who would have to move. But where?

CHAPTER FOURTEEN

KING'S CROSS

My new life began with a letter. The housing association wrote saying that it had found me a flat of my own to rent. I was 21 and this was the best news I'd had in a very long time. With my own place and my own front door, I felt I could finally take control of my life. I would shake off all the bad vibes from Camden. I would change my karma and sort my life out – again!

The flat was in a converted warehouse building just south of King's Cross Station. My only reservation was about the location. I didn't expect Kensington, and, personally, I couldn't have cared less about the druggies and the prostitutes outside, but the heart of junkie-ville in King's Cross might not have been the best place for other vulnerable people. One person who was very happy with my new location was Dad. I'd started seeing him again, and he'd agreed to help me move all my stuff in. In the end, though, it was Grandad, my uncle Daniel and Tissam who helped me move. Dunno what happened to Dad.

My new start began so well. I decided the best way to reinvent myself was to do what my mum had done and cast out all the bad shit from the past. Tissam, Chanelle and a group of true, close friends would keep me going. All the others might mess things up, so I didn't tell them my new address. Surely, if I did this, my luck would change? I don't think I realised then that when you've lived a bad life you can never really relax and that those you're trying to avoid will always find you. I guess that's why tough gang guys always look so stressed.

I got two wake-up calls about my life on my twenty-second birthday. First, my friend Alex came round in shock. He'd been arrested for something he hadn't done. I'd been at a Christmas party at a warehouse in east London when there had been a shooting. Alex had come to pick me up in his car and had been waiting outside when the police had come over and arrested him. He was still wearing that white forensic suit they make suspects wear, plus a pair of police plimsolls that were way too big for him. We sat there stunned. He was innocent, but we'd been caught up in all this crap.

The next wake-up call came that night. In the early evening, I headed out to pick up a Chinese. When I got back home, the police were waiting. As before, my first thought was pure Miss Prim: what will the neighbours think? My second thought was more direct: what the hell have I done this time?

'It's my birthday,' I said weakly as I let them into my flat, convinced that dozens of eyes were looking at us through the spyholes in my neighbours' front doors. The police couldn't have cared less.

They had got to the bottom of the credit card scam that my ex had used years ago to pay for our Florida holiday. The police talked me through it all, asked loads of questions and made me feel five years old. Then they asked me to accompany them down to the station. The walls seemed to be closing in on me. The police were so condescending: 'You're telling us you really thought he'd paid for the holiday himself?' It was embarrassing to realise how naive I'd been. 'No comment' was pretty much all I said. If my mum could have seen me, she would have been horrified. The girl who let her boyfriend pay for a fancy holiday without even asking how he'd managed to afford it was not the kind of independent woman she had raised.

'Aisleyne Horgan-Wallace, we're arresting you on suspicion of . . .' Oh, God. If she could have heard that she would have died. I nearly did.

The case came to nothing, at least not for me. I got more patronising comments before I was sent home.

'Pretty girl like you, you should choose your friends with more care,' one of the policemen told me.

'But I'm trying!' I wanted to scream. 'I've cut myself off from everyone who could mess me up. It's you that's dragging me back down into the gutter.'

For too long, I was just swamped with gloom. I was convinced that it was going to be like Bayham Street all over again. I was too embarrassed to face any of my neighbours. I convinced myself that everyone thought the worst of me. I lost the feeling of hope and confidence I'd had when I moved. So I picked up the phone and called some of the old crowd. I got ready to give everyone what they wanted.

It was nearly three years since Marc had been shot, more than a year since he had died, and I was lonely as well as miserable. I missed that cloak of protection I'd had when I'd been with him. So, despite all the problems I'd had with the police, I felt ready to jump back in with another bad boy.

The first time I saw Captain was just after my 22nd birthday from hell. I was with a group from the old days in the Litten Tree bar in Wood Green. He was wearing a fitted white jumper, blue jeans and a pair of Prada shoes. I couldn't take my eyes off him, like a schoolgirl with a crush. One thing about me: I never, ever get shy when I go out. I got shy that night. We played eyeball tennis all evening, but neither of us said a thing.

'What was that all about? Why didn't he speak to me?' I asked Tissam back at my flat, ignoring the fact that I'd not spoken to him either.

A week later, at some after-party in Finsbury Park, I was hanging out with all the late-night waifs and strays with nowhere else to go when in walked Mark Lambie with Captain. Nothing could have felt more surreal. I'd hardly seen that Mark since my Marc had been shot. I'd certainly not seen him since Marc had died. So when he came over to talk, it was pretty hard to know where to start.

Captain helped. He took control. 'Let me get you a bottle of champagne,' he said. I couldn't stop myself from smiling.

'Are you not drinking? Are you trying to get me drunk or something?' I asked when the fresh bottle arrived with just one glass. 'If you are, then you should at least tell me your name.'

'They call me Captain, but it's Curtis,' he said. 'And I don't drink!'

'I'm Aisleyne,' I told him. But he already knew that. He already knew a lot. He'd noticed me the previous week and had been asking around about me. It was good to know that he was really interested.

Curtis called me three days later. He came round to pick me up in his Mercedes. Young and dumb, I guess, but I always appreciated fine cars. It made me think of the night Dad had turned up to find me in his white Porsche. Curtis and I drove around a bit and talked that first night. It turned out that he had known my Marc as well. He'd been to Marc's house loads of times, some days turning up just after I'd left or leaving just before I arrived. We'd lived inside the same circle, but our paths had never crossed.

What I found so fascinating about Curtis was the difference between the man I got to know and the reputation he had on the street. He wasn't a tough guy or a gangster with me. He had manners; he was kind and sweet. Pretty much everything changed when I was with Curtis – just as it had done when I'd been with Marc. Even if I went somewhere on my own, I was safe because everyone knew I was Captain's girl. The trouble was, I was on my own a lot more than I'd expected.

From the start, Curtis would up and disappear for days at a time. He'd never tell me anything about where he'd been or why. I already knew that in the world we moved in women weren't supposed to ask difficult questions, but when he disappeared for two weeks, even I couldn't keep quiet. I put the word out that if I didn't hear from him it was over. So he rang me from prison. 'Why didn't you tell me you were going to jail?' I asked.

'I didn't want you to think that's the kind of person I am.'

I couldn't think of a single thing to say in reply. As a young girl, I'd always been mortified that my dad was in and out of prison. If I had to talk about my dad, I described him as this big, strong hero. Once, when I'd spun this story to some new guy I was seeing, he laughed in my face. 'He wasn't looking that hot when I saw him in Chelmsford,' he said. I cringed so much I thought I was going to die. So, crazy as it was, I completely got why Curtis wanted to keep quiet about his little absences. If he hadn't won me over already, then he'd got me now.

Curtis came straight round to the King's Cross flat when he was released a couple of months later. I let him in and got a huge burst of energy. It was like the days when my dad had turned up suddenly and exploded into the flat, full of life. Just like with Dad, there was something about Curtis's vibe that picked me up. I'd put my new career plans on hold since all the crap on my birthday, and this was just the pick-me-up I needed.

I started to party harder than ever to celebrate how good I felt about life. It took me to some pretty dangerous places – like the club where I saw someone fire a gun right next to me on the dance floor. A whole gang of us were out at some smelly warehouse party. The place was done up like a big cage. The crowd was buzzing and the music was wicked. Then, when I was dancing, a guy right beside me fired off a gun three times. The flashes of light were so shocking and so strangely beautiful that it didn't even occur to me to be scared.

'What did you do that for?' I asked the guy, as everyone else dived for cover.

'The music took me. It was the music,' was all he said.

I just agreed with him. Soon, everyone was dancing again. How did I not spot that this wasn't normal?

If bad karma had followed me back in Bayham Street, then bullets followed me in King's Cross. The next ones flew in a bar in Holborn. I was dolled up and being an airhead with my friend Carla. We were holding ridiculous shouted conversations and just buzzing with nonsense and fun.

'Did you get the shoes you wanted?' I screamed in an exaggeratedly girlie way above the noise.

'Oh, Ash, you're so funny,' she said, grabbing me and screeching with laughter.

That was when a gun went off.

'Oh, babe, why do they always do that and ruin it for everyone?' I heard myself shout to Carla. Then the music cut off and all you could hear was panic. 'Why do you always have to ruin things for everyone?' I said again, this time shouting it across the empty dance floor to where the gunman was. Then Carla and I just sat back on our little leather sofa, ready to start gossiping away again like two old ladies, while everyone else in the club edged towards the exits. Finally, some guy barrelled over, lifted the coffee table in front of us and wedged it up like a barrier. 'Get down behind here!' he shouted.

'Oi, you're not the one he's trying to get, are you?' I asked, like a suspicious old woman. Then a couple of other people who hadn't made it to the door piled over and sat on top of us behind our mini-barricade. 'Mind my hair!' I shouted. How out of it can you be?

After that little incident, friends started to joke that if I heard gunfire, I would run towards it while everyone else ran away. They had a point. I always had this mad feeling that I could calm bad situations down. Another time, out at the Scala in King's Cross, there was some major row going on across the main dance floor about 20 feet from me. A shot went off and I could see the guy with the gun as clear as anything. He was ridiculously young and so was the guy he was up against. I was determined to rush over and say my bit. 'No, boys, stop being so silly. Just put the guns down and let's all get back to enjoying our evening,' I imagined myself saying. As usual, it never even occurred to me to be scared. I was like some cross between Nanny McPhee and the Terminator. I was bizarrely convinced that my mission in life was to make peace between warring gunmen in dodgy nightclubs.

Maybe I got away with it because that protective shield that tough boyfriends wrapped around me wasn't just in my mind. But even if that was looking after me, I was about to find out that it only went so far. It only worked when I was where my boyfriends were strong. I found that out when I followed Curtis out of London to Birmingham.

We had been dating for six months when I realised I was heart and soul in love with Curtis. His spirit had got into my system. He ran through my veins. So when he was a defendant in a court case in Birmingham, I knew I had to be there too, so I went up to visit whenever I could while he was on remand. He was accused of involvement in a shooting. He hadn't done it and in the end he was found innocent, which proves justice does get done sometimes. When the trial came around, I headed north, planning to sit in on it every day. I dressed up as glam as I could each morning because I wanted to lift Curtis's spirits and look good for my man. But that first week,

Me and my proud
daddy at London Zoo.
(© aisleyne.com)

My cousin Callon and me standing
on the fireplace in Regent's Park.
(courtesy of the author)

Me and Callon again.
(courtesy of the author)

Leonie and me, hostel days.
Where are the fashion police?
Arrgh! (courtesy of the author)

On my 'ped in Islington, 2005.
(© aisleyne.com)

My darling Chanelle and me on her birthday.
I was pregnant when this picture was taken,
but I didn't know it at the time. (© aisleyne.com)

My wild clubbing days, 2004. (© aisleyne.com)

With Michael, Big Joe Egan and Joe's girlfriend Ruth,
on tour in 2005. (courtesy of Joe Egan)

Mike and me in 2005. (© aisleyne.com)

Me with Tammy and Becky at the
Rolling with the Nines film premiere.
(© aisleyne.com)

Ooh, I say! Cheeky!
Pre-boob job and pre-hair
extensions, 2005.
(© aisleyne.com)

Big Brother memories.

This is the moment I left the BB house and met Davina. Oh, the nerves when those doors opened! (© WireImage)

My best friend, thanks to the *Big Brother* House Next Door: me and Michael Cheshire at a celeb party, 2007
(© ISOIMAGES)

One of my favourite glamour shots from 2008.
(© aisleyne.com/Matt Christie)

Ooh, Matron!! My big fetish night out with Pete Bennett, 2007.
(© Edward Hirst/Newspics.com)

There are better pictures of Amy and me, but this one has been used so much that it's almost become iconic – we both look terrified! Ha! (© Xposure Press Agency)

A publicity photo for my Unique by Aisleyne clothing range, 2008 (© aisleyne.com)

From another shoot with my favourite photographer.
(© aisleyne.com/Matt Christie)

On *The Friday Night Project* with
Nikki Grahame, 2008. (© PA Photos)

Ahhh, the charming Charlie Brooker.
This was taken at a horse ranch in
Texas, 2008. (© aisleyne.com)

Me and my boy Ne-Yo when he was
touring with Pussycat Dolls, 2009.
(© aisleyne.com)

With my cousin Nico, 2009.
(courtesy of the author)

his solicitor came over to talk to me. He said I looked too much like a gangster's moll and that I wasn't doing Curtis any favours. He said I should tone it down, which I did, grudgingly.

It was all really dull. I didn't know how court cases worked. I didn't realise how often it would be postponed or how many sessions get cut short and adjourned after just a few hours. I was thrilled to at least be able to see Curtis almost every day, but when court was out I spent a lot of time bored stupid, and I ended up in more bad company.

When I told Curtis I was bored, he tried to sort it out. One of his mates, a guy called Shutter, got another mate to look after me. 'Come over to my sister's house to eat,' this new guy said. I said, 'No way, I ain't no ponce. I just wanna get a takeaway.' But he took me there anyway, saying he had to pick something up first. It turned out he hadn't cleared the invitation with his sister. 'Who let a white girl in my house?' said the big black woman when she first saw me. I took it as a joke; there was a horde of people in the kitchen and we pretty much covered every colour and mix of colours you could imagine. Why she might object to me being there was totally beyond me. But object she did. When she'd stopped shouting right at me, she and all the others started talking about me as if I wasn't there. I sat in this woman's kitchen feeling like an idiot.

'You know what? I'm going to wait outside,' I said, standing up and heading for the door.

'White bitch,' the sister said as I walked by her.

'Listen, I didn't want to come here in the first place. Your house stinks,' I fired back. Very mature, I know!

Out in the street, I realised I was screwed. I had absolutely no idea where I was. It didn't look the kind of place that you wanted to hang around. That was when it happened. One of the girls ran out of the house, grabbed the gold chain around my neck and snapped it off. I span round to try and stop her but she was back indoors pretty much before I could move. Marc had given me that chain, so it meant more than anything to me. I'd bought the cross I'd put on it myself. I went mental, banging against the door, but I couldn't get in. And where the hell was I?

I rang Shutter and he got me to describe the houses so he knew what estate I was on. 'We're coming,' he said, and rolled up with four others in a big Jag. They started bashing the door, too. 'They've all jumped over the back garden wall and I can't come out. I'm on a tag and it's past curfew,' the guy who had brought me there yelled from the top window. When the guys did get in, they found he was right. The girls were gone. My chain was gone with them.

The next day, the court did have a full session and I could tell that Curtis, over in the dock, could see the scratch marks on my chest. I was wearing a pretty low-cut top under my jacket, so he could also see that I wasn't wearing my chain.

'You OK, babe?' he mouthed at me.

'No,' I mouthed back.

My big tough boyfriend sorted it, just the way I knew he would. He made some calls that night and Shutter came round with my chain – fully repaired – the next day.

It was the day the jury was due to give its verdict on Curtis's case. I wanted to look the best I could – even if that meant looking like a gangster's moll again. Now I had my chain back, I was sure I could sparkle. I had chosen my clothes, done my hair, built up my confidence. But when I arrived at the court, I got a shock. The police wanted to speak to me. 'Is your name Aisleyne?' they kept asking. I said nothing. I didn't need the distraction; I was desperate to get into the courtroom to support Curtis. But at that moment, one of his solicitor's assistants said hello to me – by name. So the police had me. They arrested me.

It turned out the heifers from the kitchen had said I'd turned up at their house and threatened them with a gun. I got put in a police cell and I was kept there for 12 hours. It was ugly, humiliating and awful. In the first few hours, I got really low. I started to map out my future. If I got jailed, I decided, I would tell Curtis he could see other girls, just as long as he kept on loving me. I was so desperate for love back then that I thought I could cope with anything just as long as I didn't lose him.

I cried all day and I was still crying when Curtis's solicitor came to see me in the late evening. 'I've got good news and bad news,' he said. 'The good news is that Curtis was found not guilty.' I jumped for joy and thought, as long as my man is free, I am happy and can handle anything. 'The bad news is that this is really serious for you, Aisleyne.' I started to cry even more. Until that moment, I'd clung to the hope that the police believed me. Surely it was ridiculous to even think that I would go to some stranger's house in a city I didn't know and threaten a group of women I'd never met with a gun? I'd been pretty sure that I'd be allowed to go soon. But now my solicitor was saying it was serious.

In that moment, I did a lot of growing up. That was when it really hit me: I was in a police cell, a hundred miles from home, and I had absolutely no idea what was going to happen next. This was the reality of having a gangster boyfriend. It wasn't glamorous. It wasn't cool. It was fucking terrifying.

I got released just before midnight. The police said I was just some stupid, mouthy girl who'd been in the wrong place at the wrong time. Apparently, the women had wanted to use the incident to try and get rehoused off their crappy estate. Curtis was waiting outside the station in a car. His mate Dred was driving, so we could kiss and cuddle on the back seat.

'I can't go through anything like that again, Curtis,' I told him when he asked if I was OK.

'You won't have to, babe. Everything is going to be OK from now on. Nothing bad is going to happen to you. I won't let it. I'll see to it.'

It was exactly what I needed to hear. He was my strong man. He loved me and I just wanted to be loved so much. When he promised me that nothing would go wrong again, I forgot all the bad stuff. I folded my body into his as we headed south to London. I felt safe, protected, loved, the three things I'd always craved like a drug. I know now, though, that, like drugs, even such good feelings can lead to a horrific comedown.

Back in my flat in King's Cross, I was so happy. I had a rush of optimism and excitement. If Curtis loved me and if he said everything was going to be all right, then I was ready to believe him.

CHAPTER FIFTEEN

THE FASHION BUSINESS

When I first met Curtis, I'd just taken a course in buying and merchandising at the London College of Fashion, and by the time we'd been seeing each other for a few months I'd managed to get the first job I'd ever felt really passionate about. So while one side of my life was pretty chaotic during that time, I was also working hard and sure I was finally on the way to making positive changes.

I worked for a woman called Ellen. She was a brilliant, eccentric Chinese lady who ran a fashion house in Islington called Seven Cell. I'd had an interview with her after being sent by a specialist fashion recruitment agency in Oxford Street that I'd joined when I'd finished my course.

Ellen offered me an incredible opportunity. Her company was on Liverpool Road over near Angel, Islington, and I was taken on as the ultimate Girl Friday. My job was to do anything and everything. From day one, there wasn't a single thing about it I didn't love. I was convinced I could work my way all the way up to the top. The company supplied catalogues with middle-market clothes and had started to do some own-label stuff for a few stores as well. The clothes themselves were a bit mainstream for my taste, but who cared? We were a tiny team and it was a manic, pressured and wonderful environment. I had this incredible feeling the moment I arrived at work each day. I felt like I'd come home.

For the first few weeks, I just shadowed the other staff and did real gopher work – answering phones, tidying up, making tea. But when they saw I had the bug, they started to give me more chances. The best days were when I was sent to the West End to scout around for kit. I adored getting material for the designers. I loved being back around samples and reams of cotton or silk. I didn't even mind polyester! I remembered the fast-talkers on all the market stalls I'd gone to with Mum and Pete as a toddler. I did pretty well getting good prices on some of the samples Ellen and her designer, Karen, needed. It was amazing to feel appreciated. Karen was a huge inspiration. I loved her confidence and I wanted to do a job like that too.

A couple of months into my time at Seven Cell, I got my biggest boost to date. They needed a new in-house model and they asked me. It was a huge thrill because I'd never had enough confidence in my looks to consider modelling. I knew I'd never be some tall, willowy supermodel, but it didn't matter in the real world of mid-market fashion. I knew how to walk and I was an everywoman shape and size. I'd stand in the middle of them all as they created their new ranges and pinned them on me. When I had ideas, I had the guts to explain them. No one laughed me down or shut me up. The longer I stayed at Seven Cell, the more I remembered of what I'd learned from my mum. All her lessons flooded back as I watched the designers. I remembered how to draw. I realised I could still stitch. I earned a tiny, ridiculous wage, but I couldn't have cared less. I was working, not sponging.

Ellen had set up a sideline company distributing high-end beauty products with an Eastern twist. The lotions had traditional Chinese herbs in them. The bestseller was a face cream full of caviar. My colleague on that side of the business was a fun Jewish guy called Gary. He was much older than me, but our senses of humour just gelled. I'd not been with the company long when Ellen asked me to join Gary at a huge beauty show on the Isle of Man. It was a showcase for the company's biggest clients. I think I had a feeling it might not go to plan when we arrived and saw that everyone else there was a middle-aged woman. There were no men and absolutely no one under 30. The pair of us couldn't have stuck out more, but we had to get on with it.

'So what do we 'ave to do then?' Gary said as he read through an information sheet from the organiser. Then he went white. 'They want us to give a proper presentation. We need to give a speech in front of all these people.'

'Shit.'

'Exactly. Ash, you'll 'ave to do it.'

I laughed. 'No way. You're my boss. You've got to do it.'

'But I ain't a woman, I dunno what to say.'

I think I told him he should give us all the male perspective. I'd have said anything to keep him sweet.

'Well, I'm not going up on that stage on my own. You'll 'ave to come up and stand next to me,' he said.

Half an hour later, the whole room went silent as we were introduced on to the stage. There must have been hundreds of women in the room. Poor Gary was sweating buckets. So was I.

'Well, right, well, the fing abaht this stuff is . . . is . . . is that it's really good stuff,' was how he began, his cockney accent even more strangled than usual. If only he'd stopped there. But as he looked out across the room he drew inspiration from the audience. He decided he might as well give that male perspective. 'Look, all you old birds want to look younger, right?' he asked. There was a stunned silence. 'You've tried all the obvious things and nothing's worked, right?'

Somehow, he stumbled through the speech from hell. Somehow, we got off that stage without being beaten up. All I really remember is the slow handclap that greeted the end of the presentation – and the fact that we sold very little product that day.

Back in Islington, Gary and I covered up our little presentational difficulties and got back to business. I carried on dividing my days between fashion work and beauty products, and I began dreaming that one day I'd run a company like this of my own. Ellen was a total inspiration. One amazing day, she bought a house over the phone, without even looking at it. 'OK, OK, you like it? It has high ceilings? It has a garage? Then I'll buy it,' she told her estate agent as I stood, stunned, in the corner of her little office. What a fabulous woman! How I wanted to be like that.

The only bad thing Ellen did was to torture us all every lunchtime.

Her meals freaked everybody out. 'Get ready. It's bird-spit time,' Gary would whisper to me when he saw the boss heading to the tiny kitchen at the back of the building. She had a bottle of, well, bird spit (or phlegm, as she preferred to call it) each day. It was the stuff birds gob up as glue when they're making a nest, apparently, and it was supposed to be good for the skin. Ellen heated it up, stinking the place out, then drank it like very sticky soup. We were totally appalled. But, fair play, Ellen was pushing 70 and she could have passed for 40.

My other job was to handle some of the packaging and even look at a few invoices. Now, I'm not great with numbers. Ellen wasn't particularly patient about mistakes. She'd get pissed off with me. 'I'm going to explain it to you one more time, Aisleyne,' she'd begin in a tight, angry little voice. She could have told me a thousand more times and it wouldn't have made any difference. It never sank in. Fortunately, Ellen didn't hold it against me for long. In fact, she gave me a mini-promotion.

I didn't get any extra money, but I got a hell of a lot more responsibility. The beauty division had booked space at a huge cosmetics show at Olympia. Ellen pretty much gave me total control of our stand. I had to design the look of it, source the furniture, lay out all our kit and get all our marketing messages looking as good as possible. For the three days of the show, I headed out to west London at the crack of dawn to make sure it all went smoothly. When the punters came in, it was up to me to sell, sell, sell. I loved it. I did facial after facial on our stand and flogged our caviar-laden creams, face masks and collagen gels to all comers. It was a total blast.

All my life, I think, I've wanted people to say they're proud of me. Ellen said it just after the beauty show. We'd beaten all her targets and she was over the moon. At one point, I thought she might even ask me to join her for a bowl of bird-spit soup. If everything had carried on like that, I think I could have stayed at Seven Cell for years. But life was about to get in my way. I was pregnant.

• • •

I didn't realise I was having a baby until I lost it. I was five and a half months pregnant. As so often before in my life, I'd been in total denial. I'd only been aware of missing one period. Curtis was on remand up in Birmingham at the time and I'd put it down to stress about that and my new job. What with everything that I was trying to deal with, I wasn't surprised that my body was all over the place.

It was a Saturday afternoon and I was alone in my flat when the first waves hit me. It was an immense wall of pain that came from nowhere. In seconds, I felt delirious with it and was having cramps and contractions. My mind was spaced out and something told me I had to try and float above it to survive. Something else told me I had to get help. I was fumbling for my mobile phone, aware for the first time of how small the buttons were. I started to cry with frustration as I was shaking so much I couldn't even unlock the keypad. That was when my doorbell went. I was going to be saved. I couldn't get to the hall, but I was at least able to cry out.

'Ash, what's up with you?' It was an old friend we all called Soldier. As I screamed again, I realised I was bleeding. Loads and loads, more and more. It was horrible and it wouldn't stop. Soldier was still buzzing the door but I couldn't get to it. I was barely conscious I was in so much pain and I couldn't understand what was happening. I think I was in denial even then about it all, thinking, if I ignore this, the pain will go. If I pretend I'm fine, it'll stop.

Somehow, I made it to the door. Soldier's a tough guy, but he nearly fainted when he saw the blood. He called an ambulance while I lurched back to the bathroom. That was when I gave birth. I still couldn't really grasp what had happened. I was scared and delirious with the pain.

I was in hospital for just under a week. That first night, I didn't think they would ever stop the bleeding, or that the pain would ever end. I'd lost so much blood that they lined up a transfusion, though in the end I managed to pull through with just an intravenous drip.

'Will the father or your family be visiting you?' the midwife asked. I couldn't reply. How could I say that the baby's father was in jail, my father was probably on his way there too, and my mum didn't seem to care if I was alive or dead? What kind of girl had a crap life like that? I was too embarrassed to say another word.

Soldier got a message to Curtis in Birmingham and he called while my cousin Nico was at my side on my last day in hospital. We had the most awful, emotional conversation. I loved him. I couldn't bear that I had lost his child. Both of us cried, though neither of us really knew what to say.

By the time I was allowed home, Curtis had arranged things, the way he always did. He had set up a visit with a priest for me. I headed to Birmingham and the two of us sat with the priest in a quiet little room. Curtis and I held each other for a long time, then we talked about life and death and grief. I just felt so ill and I cried from start to finish of the visit. But the priest was wonderful. He was quite young, but he was calm and wise and seemed to know exactly what to say and when.

But then he asked, 'Did you have a funeral for the baby?' That brought me up short. I'd given birth in the toilet. How could I tell him what I had done with our baby's body? I could never say those words out loud again. 'Perhaps it would help if you named your baby,' the priest said, finally. It did help. We named our baby Skye.

Sadly, since then I've had several more miscarriages. The first one was the worst, the most painful and traumatic, because the pregnancy was so far along. While the physical pain was less each time, the shock and sense of loss were not. In some ways it was even harder because I often felt really alone. There is always someone who can try to help you through, though, no matter how isolated you feel, and there are contact details for the Miscarriage Association at the end of this book.

• • •

I handed in my notice at Seven Cell shortly after the miscarriage. They had sent flowers and been really kind to me, but I'd missed so many days' work while I'd been recovering that I felt a bit of a fraud about turning up again. I lost all my confidence and couldn't see myself walking through the doors of the workshop again. Then there was something else. I realised that I had been pregnant almost every day that I had been working for the company. I felt as if every aspect of the job I had loved was associated with the baby I had lost. I couldn't get my head round that, so I walked away.

The only good thing that happened in the weeks that followed was Curtis beating the charge in Birmingham. I had a friend round to my flat just after he'd been released and I was celebrating with her. We had loud music on and were dancing because I was so happy to have him back. That was when it happened.

Curtis was downstairs, trying to get away from the police. He rang my buzzer and my mobile, but I didn't hear them. Then he shot a gun into the door of my building to try and get in that way. I never heard that either. With the police getting closer, he then tried to hijack a black cab to escape, but he got caught. All while I was dancing.

When I went out that night, I stood looking at our damaged door. 'What the fuck has happened?' I thought. I was in my own little world. It never crossed my mind that it might have anything to do with me. I just got on my moped and headed off across town, wondering where on earth Curtis was.

Back at the flat that night, I had visitors. A big group of white guys – police. I let them into my living room and they were asking questions, not naming anyone, just trying to insinuate that I knew what they were talking about. Then they searched my flat. 'So, you don't know him, do you?' they said, all sarky, holding up a picture of me and Curtis kissing. I was frozen inside because I knew something serious was up.

The police wouldn't say much, but I spoke to the neighbours and pieced together what had happened at our front door. Curtis would eventually be given eight years for firearms offences. But I couldn't judge him. Life moulds people. I knew this life wasn't the one I wanted, but it wasn't his fault; it wasn't what he wanted either. So how could I judge the only person in the world who loved me? I was there with him. I was in his life, for better or for worse. I was his strength and he was mine.

After Curtis was arrested, Tissam came round to talk me through it all. 'So how are you, babes?' Sitting in my flat, I was cold as ice. 'You need to get away,' Tissam said. 'We should have a holiday. You need some way to clear your head.' But we didn't have any money. Tissam probably couldn't have gone anyway. She had her lovely baby boy Kieran, my godson, to look after. 'You could go out tonight, take your mind off it,' she said. But I suddenly knew that was the very last thing I needed to do. I mustn't, just mustn't, slip back into the old ways. All the bad influences would still be out there. I would be going nowhere, dragging myself down.

'I'm going to get another job,' I said suddenly. I would work and save and fight to make a better future for my man and me. I would do whatever it took to make sure I had a better life waiting for him when he got out.

'You're going back to the land of the bird-spit soup?'

It felt good to smile. 'Not quite. I've got a better idea.'

When I'd set up that beauty stand at Olympia, I'd been dazzled by the beautiful promotions women – and the little group of equally good-looking men – who worked on the stalls. I'd chatted to some of them between facials. 'It's great money and it's good work,' they'd told me. It turned out there was a whole freelance promotions circuit I'd never even heard of. They got paid to do shows, launch things, act like enthusiastic members of the crowd and make parties go well. Their job was to smile, chat, socialise and sell stuff. They did a bit of travelling, spending the night in hotels around the country and all over Europe. Why had it taken me so long to realise how great that sounded?

CHAPTER SIXTEEN

———————●———————

JOINING THE PROMO GIRLS

'Hello, free goodie bag for you. Free goodie bag. Hello, free goodie bag.' My first gig in the promotions world was outside Edgware Road Tube station one Monday morning at 7.30 a.m. I was wearing an embarrassingly bad corporate anorak, handing out a lousy product and trapped in a terrible location. I absolutely loved it.

Next up came coffee machines. I stood on windy streets trying to make out that these ridiculously complicated machines were the most exciting things in the world. I loved that too. I'd scored jobs right from my first interviews. I like to think the agencies could tell I was determined, keen and reliable. I was also tough enough to laugh off the occupational hazards. I couldn't care less what the commuters thought if I needed to get the Tube at 7 a.m. in a tiny black minidress and high heels because I was working a show in Wembley. I'd get an early-morning bus in an evening dress to do a gig in a hotel and I wasn't remotely bothered what the other passengers thought about me. All that mattered was that I was working. That fact lit me up from the inside.

One of the great things about the work was meeting so many different girls on the various jobs – and finding that most of the time we all got along. It was brilliant to socialise with a completely new crowd. We were all sorts, mostly in our 20s but some quite a bit older. Some wanted to be actresses or singers, others were super-hot models. Some were earning money while they did degrees at university, others were saving up so they could travel the world or set up their own businesses. The one common factor seemed to be that none of them lived in hostels, woke up to find armed police in their rooms or got arrested while waiting to see their boyfriends get sent down for crimes they hadn't done.

Earning clean money of my own was fantastic, too. It felt like money I could really spend. So of course I did. I bought shoes, clothes, better skincare products, masses of stuff for my house. Sure, I'd not really liked posh Jennie in the Camden hostel, but I knew she had good taste, so I copied her and got a glass teapot of my own. I bought one of the crazy coffee machines (at a big discount) and started to have my new friends round for dinner. Another big relief was being able to talk about work with the other promo girls. This was the one subject that had been off limits all my life. My dad, Marc, Curtis, the boys in the gangs and the girls in the hostels – none of them ever talked about jobs. But suddenly I realised it was OK to have ambition and to want something more from life. Some people might have thought I was boring – *Ab Fab*'s Saffy all over again – but I actually wanted to talk about saving. I wanted foundations under my life. I got a thrill out of having a busy work diary. I loved knowing I had jobs booked in for weeks and even months ahead. I got a reputation at the agency as the girl who wouldn't say no – in a good way, of course.

In my first six months of promotions, I did it all. Free newspapers and magazines, chocolate bars, energy drinks, Lynx deodorants, music vouchers. I did the motorbike and car shows, dressed up in Lycra alongside all the other hot girls. I wore naff pinafores and handed out food samples in shopping centres. I bigged up the crowds at video game releases and sprayed perfume at people in department stores. I went round the country in a van selling coffee machines, getting a huge thrill out of staying in Travelodges – where I got an even bigger thrill out of taking the shampoo and soap from the bathroom. The whole thing was like being a kid in a candy shop. Back in London, I poured drinks at press parties and at loads of big charity shows. I got to go to hotels on Park Lane, skyscrapers in the City, even the Savoy on the Strand.

Of course, I wasn't a total angel. I loved ducking and diving. It was brilliant to hang out with the other girls and find ways to bunk off. Just grabbing ten minutes to kick the high heels off and get some fresh air was a real achievement at some of the huge trade shows. The guys who put the stands together and pulled them apart at the end of the weekend were cool. They were even keener than we were on finding ways to work the minimum possible hours for the maximum possible pay. I loved getting tips off them.

The hierarchy of the promo world appealed to me as well. I'd always wanted more structure in my life, and it was really good to be able to measure my achievements and see the progress I was making. When you're just leafleting, you're at the bottom of the ladder. If those were the only jobs you could get, it was bad news. Leafleting was the toughest gig and we all knew it. I'd lie all the time about why I was doing those jobs. 'I was just bored today. I only agreed to do it this morning because I didn't have anything else on,' I'd say, or, 'They asked me so nicely that I couldn't say no.' My favourite was: 'I'm covering for a friend.' Handing out samples was pretty shit, too, especially the early-morning rush-hour jobs outside Tube stations. But at least if the product was half decent you could leave with a nice stash of it in your bag. I didn't have to buy my own breakfast cereal for months after one job and I could have taken a bath in all the sports drinks I got on another.

The best jobs were at the big trade shows and the parties. I loved being the face of some product on a car or bike stand. I didn't even mind the pervy guys who wanted you to lean just that little bit further over when they took their pictures. Mingling at posh hotel parties was even better. If they were mobbed, then the time normally flew, so you felt like you earned your money even faster. If the events were flops, then you got the chance to talk to the organisers or the handful of punters who had turned up. Sometimes I'd get so involved in those conversations I forgot I was working. 'Where the hell is the girl with the drinks?' I'd think as I launched into yet another anecdote about my past or plan for my future. It was amazing I got away with it for as long as I did.

What I loved about working so hard was that I was building up a future for me and Curtis. I was sure that if I could get enough money together, we could have a great life when he got released. I'd have enough to set us up in business or something. Anything to stop him going back to crime. I talked about it all the time when I visited him. Then I went on about all the posh hotels, fancy parties and flash events I'd worked at. Once in a while, I'd stop to draw breath and ask him how he was getting on. Then it was back to my stories. No wonder he thought he had to come up with something very special to get my attention. And, respect to him, he did manage to grab the spotlight the day he proposed.

He did it in Pentonville prison where he was awaiting trial. We were getting to the end of my visit and had stood up to say goodbye. He wanted to stretch the rules, as usual, with a bit of a hug and kiss. He told me how much he wanted us to be together, how I was everything to him and how much he needed me to stay true while he was inside. I was looking around the big, harshly lit visiting room and worrying that the guards were going to have something to say about the hug when he delivered his best line: 'Aisleyne, you know you're going to marry me, innit.'

His head was buried in my hair so it was a bit muffled. I started to pull away to ask him what the hell he had just said and he pulled me closer. We ended up in some sort of loved-up wrestling match. He'd got me in a sort of headlock, but a nice one, if you can imagine that. 'I'm not joking. You're going to marry me, innit,' he repeated. I have to say that wasn't how I'd imagined things when I was a little girl. But to be fair, I wasn't exactly romantic myself. I certainly didn't say, 'I do.'

'Let go of my head,' was all I could come up with. Not bad, under the circumstances. I finally got free as the guards started to close in on us.

'What the hell happened to going down on bended knee?' I asked as we sat back down at our plastic-covered table.

'I dunno about all that. But you heard me, right?'

'I heard you.'

'So what do you say?'

'Yeah, of course I will,' I said.

Romance in the traditional sense of the word might have been dead that day in Pentonville, but it felt romantic to me all the same. So I threw myself into our engagement. With prisons being a bit low on jewellery stores, it was up to me to choose our rings. Curtis paid for mine, a big single-diamond ring, while I got him a Cartier love ring. We exchanged them in Chelmsford prison, where Curtis, still on remand, had been transferred. We began to make some plans. If he got off, we decided, we would go to Trinidad to see his family that year, then get married on a beach somewhere the following year. But when his case came to trial and he got eight years, we had to think again. I was still going to be loyal to the one man in the world who loved me and I loved back. He was my only family and if I had to wait a bit longer, then I'd wait. Who cared if it was going to be the longest engagement on record?

Back outside, I carried on working the promotions circuit. I was making some really cool friends, but while I loved all the girl talk about dodgy boyfriends, I could never quite bring myself to say that mine was inside – and looked set to stay there for some time. I spun a few lies to explain why I was always free to work. My boyfriend works abroad, he's away on a big contract up north – all the things I used to say about my dad when I was a girl.

Some of the older girls were buying their first flats. They told me that in a few years time I might have a shot at buying my King's Cross place from the housing association. I became obsessed with that. Aisleyne Horgan-Wallace, homeowner. That sounded bloody fantastic.

The only trouble was, the promotions world was changing. After my first year in the business, it seemed to explode. More and more girls heard about the opportunities and started signing up for all the agencies. I still got work because the bookers trusted me, but my wages fell. Hostess jobs started to pay samplers' wages. Sampling jobs paid the same as the old leafleting gigs. The poor sods outside the rush-hour Tube stations with the leaflets were really being screwed. I needed a new direction and I decided to take the logical next step. If I looked good enough to sell some crappy product in a shop or trade show, then couldn't I look good enough to sell myself on camera? Watch out, Jordan. I was ready to take on the world of glamour.

CHAPTER SEVENTEEN

●

GLAMOUR

Jordan didn't really need to worry about me. When I started modelling in 2003, she'd been the queen of the scene for a while. I didn't quite have her confidence, or her implants, but she was a perfect role model. Sometimes you heard a few jealous girls telling some tale of how they reckoned she was a bitch, but mainly you heard she was a grafter. If nothing else, I decided, I could copy that. But how could I get started?

Glamour girls were even more secretive than promo girls. They reckoned they were well above all of us and they were desperate to stop us climbing onto their ladder. 'Well, I suppose you could *try*,' they'd tell me, reeking with negativity and looking me up and down like I was the world's biggest loser. 'You might get something in porn, honey. Or have you done that already?' one top bitch asked me at a bike show when I tried to tap her for her agent's phone number.

When I struck out on my own, I realised that, like every other wannabe model, I needed work to get pictures but I couldn't get pictures without work. That was unless I took up some very pervy-sounding offers. So I took up some very pervy-sounding offers. The first was from a man out in Canning Town who was looking for models. I got his number from a free Internet site. Something about that might have convinced me he was a chancer, but he said he had a proper photographic studio. He was offering to help girls get great portfolio pictures while he perfected his craft, something like that. I called him up. I didn't like or trust him one bit, but two days later I headed east. I ended up in his bedroom.

'You said you had a studio,' I said, trying to sound mouthy and cross, when in fact I was terrified. I'd turned down a day at a craft fair in Islington to do this. Was I going to end up chopped up in little pieces, my death posted on the Internet?

'It is a studio. Trust me,' he said.

Yeah, right, I thought. I was boiling hot in the room. The door was shut, but the main thing that kept me there was the fact that we seemed to be in some kind of shared house. I was hoping that someone nearby would hear if I had to scream. I didn't want to even consider the idea that whoever else was around might be in on the act, ready to set up the webcam while my new friend chopped me up.

'Just relax,' the guy told me. 'I'm going to do some great pictures.' And, to be fair, he did have a hell of a lot of lighting and kit in his bedroom. That was why we were both sweating so much.

All the lights and umbrellas were focused on his bed. Behind that was the only other thing that suggested the man was a professional not a perv. It was a roll of pure-white photographic backdrop that covered the wallpaper and ran down over the headboard of the bed. 'He won't want to get blood on that,' I thought, feeling just the tiniest bit more confident. Then I realised that to get in front of that backdrop I would have to get onto this man's bed. Apart from anything else, I wasn't convinced that the sheets were very clean. Why on earth hadn't I just gone to the craft show?

'Just relax, babe. You want the pictures, don't you?' And that was the whole point. That is the power that dodgy photographers have over young models. I got with the programme, told myself it was now or never and got on the guy's bed. For the next hour, I leaned back, I tossed my hair, I looked over my shoulders and I draped myself all over his sheets, clean or not. And you know what? The results weren't half bad. A creepy, crappy little back bedroom really can be transformed into something pretty professional when you blank out all the seedy surroundings. I left that house with my first set of pictures on a shiny new disk. The guy said he would work on a few of the best ones and I could come and collect them in a day or two. 'You've got something,' he said as he burned them onto his computer. On the one hand, I thought he'd probably have said that to Shrek if he thought he could get a shag out of it, but on the other I felt proud. I held onto those words for quite a long time. If he was right, then I was finally on my way.

When I went to collect the touched-up pictures from Canning Town, the guy had really come through for me. He'd done some tricks with the colours and faded out a few flaws. The black-and-white ones were pretty classy, though I say so myself. He didn't charge me anything and he never even came on to me. In all the years ahead, he never sold the pictures or his story to the papers either. I just wish I still had his number.

I kept on doing promotions while I slowly built up a portfolio of glamour pictures. Getting photos done became easier as I got a bit more confidence and experience. I met a lot of people at shows who did pictures. The car and bike expos and the big product launches were the best for meeting photographers. They were always asking to do extra pictures and that worked just fine for me. Another guy I found online did some shots for me at his flat in Highgate. He didn't have a proper studio either. I was starting to wonder if anyone did. But he got me at just the right time. I'd got a bit more confidence and I was OK getting changed in front of him. I'd brought a whole bag of clothes so that we could make it look like the pictures had been taken at lots of different shoots. He talked me through every detail. It was irritating at first, but it worked. He told me how he wanted me to pose and some of it sounded bloody stupid. I was terrified of looking sleazy or cheesy. I kept thinking about my mum. But the results? On the screen, most of it looked OK.

Next up was this German guy who charged me for his work. I didn't have much cash back then and I didn't want to pay, but he'd been talked about a lot on the circuit and it turned out he was good. Then there was the posh man in Kensington who did the shots for all the high-class escort girls. He had great backgrounds and the best lights. Working with him felt like a real step up. I just wished he hadn't kept going on about how much some of his other clients earned. 'You don't have to do full sex. You can keep it safe,' he kept saying. 'Lots of the guys are OK, really. Call me if you want to try it. You can make double what you make now just by working a few nights a month.'

I said I'd bear it in mind. I added his shots to my collection and then selected all my favourites. I got on the case and started to email them to the papers, the agencies, the fixers and the lads' mags. Now all I needed to do was wait for the job offers to come in.

'Look, if they want you, you'll know about it straight away. If you haven't heard so far then, well, there must be a problem.' Was that just one more example of an existing glamour girl trying to put me off and discourage the competition? If so, then it worked. This girl I'd met on a promo gig had done loads of magazines, and I think I might have recognised her. She reckoned she was about to sign for a calendar. She was blonde, she had a great body and a really dirty look in her eyes. I wanted to get every bit of advice and contact information I could out of her. She wanted me to jump off a cliff.

That was probably why she battered my confidence and then told me to get in touch with so many lousy agencies. She gave me a list of all the cowboy firms. The ones who promise the world in return for a big upfront fee. She was probably on commission. My new friend Becky saved me. She was a wonderful Welsh girl who did glamour as well as promotions, which was how we'd met. She put me on shark alert so that I could try and avoid the worst of the rip-off merchants. But if getting a portfolio together was tough, then finding my first few paying jobs was even tougher. That was when things got really seedy.

The websites were the worst. They hardly pay any money, they let almost anyone lift their pictures, and no prizes for guessing that the locations were never very clean. I did my first shoot in a studio bang in the middle of Covent Garden. It's funny how 'lingerie' sounds so much classier than underwear, that 'swimwear' can sound exotic. Of course, it's all really just bras and panties with a posher label. But you know what? I was cool with all of it. In fact, I loved it. Hand on heart, who doesn't want to look sexy? I adored showing off and being paid compliments. The only thing I wish I'd known was that it would always be so bloody cold. That overheated back bedroom on my first shoot was a total one-off. From that moment on, whether it was wind machines or ice cubes on your nipples, they were always finding a way to make me freeze. If they want you looking hot and steamy, they spray water on you.

After a few shoots, I also got over a little hang-up I had: wearing other girls' kit or being given clothes that who knows how many others had already worn. I would refuse to put stuff on unless I was 100 per cent sure that it had been cleaned. Do I really want to think too much about that, even today? Not really. But it was all just like getting on that first bed and getting on with it. You do what you do. You hope for the best.

'Can you repeat that address for me again?' My first really weird job was out in the middle of nowhere. I had to get a train from London Bridge and then a cab at the other end. 'I'll tell you what,' the photographer had told me, 'we'll get someone to meet you at the station. She's called Lou. You won't be able to miss her.' He wasn't lying. Lou looked like she'd come straight out of some sort of whorehouse. She was wearing an extremely short, extremely tight skirt, fishnets and a bra top that looked to be several sizes too small, all topped off with dodgy make-up and peroxide extensions. We were in deepest suburban Kent in broad daylight. I was horrified, so God knows what all the commuters thought.

'So what kind of pictures do they want?' I asked as she drove us through the town.

'Interesting ones,' she said, in a fake American accent.

Oh dear, oh dear.

Lou parked alongside a big metal fence on a derelict-looking industrial estate. We tottered over towards a warehouse, where what looked like a crazy homeless guy was shooting at pigeons with an air pistol. He turned out to be our photographer.

'OK, the ropes are over there.'

Oh, God, those weren't words I had ever really wanted to hear. But it was that kind of shoot. The photographer and I had to tie Lou up and then sit her in some sort of director's chair. My job was to pretend we were playing spin the bottle and, of course, the deal was that we lost a layer of clothes after every spin.

For all the weirdness, I never felt in any danger out there. We'd agreed on the phone that it wasn't a hardcore shoot and that I wouldn't go fully topless, let alone nude. Lou did and she got an extra £120, I think. Anyway, the photographer was happy with the clothes I'd brought and with the different layers I was prepared to lose. I gave my hair and make-up the once-over while air-pistol boy got his lights together. Then we were off.

That was when it got a little weird. It was maybe five or so minutes and a few spins of the bottle later that a second photographer turned up. I never heard him arrive; I could just hear, then see, the second set of flashes fire off from his camera. Then through the flashes and below this new camera, I vaguely made out some bizarre white objects. What the hell were they? A few more spins down the line, I got it. They were the photographer's teeth. The biggest, brightest, most crooked Bugs Bunny teeth I had ever seen.

'You're not getting into this enough, Aisleyne,' air-pistol boy shouted from behind his camera. 'I want to see you getting turned on.' I met Lou's eyes. She gave a trace of a smile. 'I get turned on by the money,' she shouted back at our boss. The cash did help. I can't quite remember, but I think I got £500. It was my biggest photographic wage to date. So I left that warehouse feeling pretty good. To be honest, I'm not even bothered that the shoot came back to haunt me and got re-released when I was in the *Big Brother* house. It's a good lesson for any new model, though. Be warned, girls: everything you do in the dark comes out eventually, like it or not.

One lesson I learned at the time was about model release forms. If you sign, then you collect your few hundred quid but you lose all control over the pictures. You can't make any more money if they suddenly become hot property. Ben, one of the guys I did some wild stuff with early on in my glamour days, sold a set for £50,000 when I was in *Big Brother*. I think I only got a few hundred pounds when I posed for him – big mistake. As if losing out on the cash isn't bad enough, you don't know where the pictures you've signed away will be used, nor do you know what kind of words they'll write alongside them. I saw plenty of girls in tears because they'd had their faces put alongside really hardcore porn stories in magazines. There were terrible speech bubbles saying what they wanted guys to do to them or what they'd supposedly had a total blast doing the night before.

Saying no to release forms isn't easy, I'll admit. You can get bounced off some jobs or see your pay packet shrink. So you need to decide what works for you. Just remember, everyone in glamour lies. Including the girls. 'No, there's nothing happening today. It's totally dead. No one's hiring,' they'd say, tarting themselves up for a casting. 'The *Nuts* shoot got cancelled. They're using old pictures instead,' they'd say, heading right off there the moment they hung up on your call.

If I hadn't had Becky and some promotions contacts, I don't think I'd have even heard about half the jobs I did. Several of the big promo firms had glamour arms, and because they knew me, they got me in on some shoots before the crowd. Becky, meanwhile, had some more mainstream contacts who took me on. I also got back into the rag trade, doing some very minor catwalk shows, really just private fashion stuff for a few up-and-coming designers, and working as a house model for some Brick Lane and Commercial Road clothes companies, just like at Seven Cell.

When I write all this down, it seems like my first few years in glamour modelling were totally cool, but it didn't always feel like that at the time. Sure, I made a decent amount of money, but I never really put down roots in the industry. I started to feel lonely, too. Glamour was very different from promotions. We'd had our rows and rivalries in the promo world. We'd been *The Osbournes*, not *The Waltons*, but it had still felt a bit like a big happy family. In glamour, your relationships were totally dysfunctional. All the girls were chasing the same jobs, so we kept secrets and built up walls. No one said when any castings were being held. No one said who had found them work. And everyone lied about what they earned. Throw in all the new girls who were starting to do pictures for free because they believed all the dirty old men photographers spinning lies, and it was dog eat dog – almost literally, when you look at some of the pictures. (Did I mention how bitchy it all was?)

Right from the start, I'd said that I wouldn't do full-frontal topless. One reason was that my mum's voice was always in my head whenever I was pushed to go for it. 'God's going to be watching you. You'll be punished if you go even further from his light.' Sometimes I don't think I'll ever lose that voice, but maybe that's no bad thing. Another reason I covered up was that even then I had a bit more business sense than most people expected. I had an instinct that the longer I could hold out, the higher the pictures' value would go. That's one message I'd give anyone else starting out in glamour today: timing is everything. You want to hold things back as long as you can, though not so long that no one's interested any more. I never said it was easy!

Nor is it easy to stick to your guns. 'You could earn double this if you show everything,' the photographers and the agencies all say, time after time, when they talk you through each job. It was like earning double in the short term if you signed away your picture rights: a gamble that every girl has to make her own mind up about.

My final reason for keeping it all relatively clean? I had a feeling that my boobs weren't big enough. I thought I might as well keep my options open, so I saved up for a boob job. I researched it like a university project because I was terrified of going to some Sweeney Todd type who would butcher me and leave me looking like some kind of mutant. I wanted a surgeon who knew what they were doing, showed me their past results and gave a shit about their patients. That was a lot harder to find than I'd thought.

I found one guy who was supposedly pretty good and who I'd heard had done loads of glamour girls. I was left speechless. I don't think he looked up from his desk once. I could have been a bloke in a dress with a high-pitched voice for all he knew. To my mind, all he did was run a production line for women with more money than sense. I couldn't get out of his office fast enough. I'm not sure he even noticed I'd gone.

In the end, I found my man. He'd been doing operations since before I was born. I saw him in his offices in Harley Street, and he spent nearly two hours with me before I'd even signed anything and before I'd paid him a penny. He talked more about what I shouldn't do than about what I should. He advised me not to go too big, and he just seemed really genuine and caring. So off I went to sign up with his lovely assistant. I paid £4,000 to go from a B to an E when he was next at Highgate Hospital. I'd always wanted it and I've never regretted it. I was so pleased with how the operation turned out. When I came out of the *Big Brother* house, Davina told me on live TV that they were the best fake boobs she'd ever seen, and women often write to me to ask who did the op. Of course, it was done under general anaesthetic, so I didn't know anything about it. You do go pale when you come round and see the stitches and the bruises. I felt a bit sick when I realised that these funny sacks were in my chest for ever, too. But, hey, they were going to change my life, right?

So did my new boobs make me rich and famous? Not really. Jordan still didn't have too much to worry about. I started off doing some shoots with guys I'd worked with before, when I'd worn padded bras and put chicken fillets in. Now I could be 'natural' and that was a bit of a selling point for a while. Before and after shots get some people going, so I did OK out of that till people got bored of it.

Then it was just back to the grindstone. I worked it. I'd always known I wouldn't be the prettiest girl on the glamour circuit, not by a long way, but I turned up. I was always on time and I put the hours in. I wasn't doing drugs and getting wasted the night before a big shoot. I bounced back from all the bad aspects of it. The castings and the rejections eat away at you. It's an endless, unforgiving beauty pageant. You can't pretend that you're not being judged. Are you thin enough, tall enough, blonde enough? How's your skin? Are your tits full enough, is your smile OK, do you have that dirty look in your eye?

Porn films seemed to have taken over the world by the time my new tits and I were fully back on the circuit. I got more and more offers to do movies every day. But I was never crossing that line, and not just because I had my mum's voice in my head telling me to keep away. Once you've done porn, you can never take the images back. So I stopped at a few pretty tame webcasts, all of which were distinctly odd.

For the weirdest one, I was paired up with this real babe of a girl and we sat down at replica school desks. Warning bells were going off in every part of my mind, but this wasn't some sexy schoolgirl scene. People were asking us questions over the Internet: history, general knowledge, current affairs – none of which was really my strong suit. You'd expect we'd be told to start taking things off every time we got a question wrong, but that wasn't the deal. No, on this site wrong answers meant we got gunged. We were covered in buckets full of cold, slimy green stuff. Was it supposed to be sexy? Or was the thrill just that they were humiliating a pair of dumb blondes? When I'd been a little girl I'd always wanted to be on one of those Saturday morning TV shows where the guests got covered in slime. Now I was finally getting to do it – but with a bit of a weird twist. It was easier to see the attraction of the mud fights in bikinis. I did my share of those, though I drew the line at oil wrestling because I was worried about twisting my ankle. I could still surprise people by coming over all sensible at the most unlikely moments.

Parties are the big perk for glamour girls, and after a while on the scene I was ready to take full advantage. I loved getting invitations to cool places. And a free drink is a free drink, right? Better still, parties were where you looked good and made connections. Even if they didn't bring in any new work, it was a chance to make some decent friends. I got lucky with my invites from the start. It was brilliant to hang out with people who were really going places. There was one night I was in a club with the Black Eyed Peas. They were fabulous and I really hit it off with them. We hit club after club that night, darting around London in their tour bus.

The more parties I went to, the more people I recognised and the more recognised me – including some of the paparazzi. 'What's your name, darling?' one of them yelled one night when I walked into Kabaret and then Faces with Ne-Yo. He's a great guy, so talented. But what was that? The photographer wanted *my* name? Really? He asked for it again, so I guessed he was serious. 'Aisleyne! Aisleyne!' I sang out. I think I might have been uncool enough to have spelled it out for him. But what a rush next time the paps were out when this one guy remembered and his mates started yelling out for me too. I know it's their job to remember everyone from the A-list down, but I was blown away. It's not curing cancer or winning the Nobel Prize or anything, but the London paps knew my name! I felt as if I'd achieved something that night. I didn't come down for days.

It was good to have something to smile about, because in the back of my mind I was getting worried about the future. All models have a shelf life and for glamour models the best-before dates come round even faster. I'd already joined the game later than most and sometimes I felt about 100 years old when I saw the really young girls at shoots. I was 25 and I wanted to pull together as much money as possible before the phone stopped ringing. For a while, I started to think about setting up my own modelling or promotions agency – a dream that still flits in and out of my mind today. What I really wanted was to keep my life stable. I knew I couldn't let any of the heartache from my past distract me while I figured out my next move. But that was easier said than done. Curtis was about to be allowed out on day release. And I'd just got a letter from my mum.

CHAPTER EIGHTEEN

LOSING MUM

My prison visits had been getting a lot harder to handle. I'd long since realised that being locked up plays with your mind big time. Once, I left my phone in my car and came back to find 13 missed calls from Curtis. Out of nowhere, he was convinced that I was seeing some other man right at that moment. In fact, I'd been popping in and out of all the Turkish shops on Green Lanes buying fruit and veg. My life was nowhere near as exciting as he thought.

Our other big problem was dealing with the way our lives had changed. He'd never liked the idea of his girlfriend doing glamour pictures. But then I'd never liked the idea of him doing time. When he called in summer 2005 to say he was about to be allowed every other Saturday out, we knew we had to call a truce.

'Well, babe, I'm back.' I got the sharpest flashback when Curtis was sitting on my new orange sofa in King's Cross. It was like Dad coming back into Mum's world. And that summer, I needed him more than ever. Because Mum had got in touch with me.

I'd recognised the handwriting on the letter the moment I saw it. I picked it off my hall floor and walked into the living room with it. All I could think of were the good times with Mum, the years when she had been this manic creative genius, when she'd filled our home with crazy friends and seemed able to take on the world. Whatever I'd been hoping for, the letter wasn't it. Apart from the fact that my name was on it, it was so impersonal that it could have been written to almost anyone. I'd sent back a letter full of love, saying how sorry I was for leaving her, saying I thought I'd been the latest person to betray her and that I wanted to start all over again. She'd replied with a short, sharp note saying I was pathetic, that I didn't know a thing and that I was a stupid little girl who would never grow up.

'See what you think of this,' I said, handing the letters to Curtis.

'That's harsh, babe,' Curtis said. Then I let go. I realised I had kept my past secret for so many years. I'd never told any of the promotions or glamour girls about losing my mum. They knew I'd lived in a few hostels, but I never really said why. With Marc gone, I realised, very few people understood my full story. Curtis came through as an amazing listener that day. I got such a lift from talking and getting it off my chest at last.

'So what do you want to do, babe?' he asked when evening came.

'Do?' I didn't think there was anything I could do. Hadn't Mum just made it perfectly clear she didn't want to see me? What do you do about that?

'You want to see her, don't you?'

I looked around the room. 'How can I see her? She doesn't even like me. She walked away from me at a funeral. I wouldn't know what to say.'

'Well, let's find out. It's been cutting you up all this time, babes. And she's your mum. You need to make peace.'

So Curtis became my strength. He took charge. 'We're going to see her next Saturday and if she's not in, we'll stay outside her flat until she is. You need your mum in your life, babe. When she sees you, she's going to want you. Trust me, babes. We can work this out.'

When Saturday came, Mum didn't answer her buzzer. But someone else came out of the building and let me into the hall. I headed up that same old staircase. It was the first time I'd been there since Mum had changed the locks on me when I was in the first hostel. I didn't want to think about that rejection again.

'Mum, are you in there? It's me, Aisleyne.' I knocked because there wasn't a bell. There was no response, though through the door I could have sworn I could hear the sound of a radio. 'Are you in, Mum?' I looked through the letter box and realised I was right about the radio. Through the little rectangle of light, I could see my old hall. More memories flooded back.

'Ash, if she's not in, we'll just wait downstairs until she comes back.'

'But it's your one day out. We can't waste it on that.'

'It's OK.'

So we sat in my car in the street. We talked, we joked, we listened to the radio and tried to pretend this was a perfectly normal thing to be doing. Then, after maybe three long hours, I saw her. She was leaving the building. So she had been in the flat all along.

'Go up to her,' Curtis said.

'I can't.'

'Ash, it's what we're here for. You have to do this. I'll be right with you.'

Somehow, I knew that would be a mistake. 'Stay in the car. I don't want to scare her.'

I got out of the car and crossed the street. 'Mum,' was all I could say. 'Mum?' She absolutely exploded.

'Oh, for goodness' sake! Can you not just leave me alone?'

She picked up the pace and headed towards an alleyway that led down towards Hampstead Road.

'Mum, I just wanted to talk to you. You've been writing to me.'

'Just leave me alone.'

'But what have I done, Mum? I haven't seen you for years. Please talk to me, tell me what's wrong.'

She looked at me in disgust and said, 'No. Just leave me alone. For once in your life, just leave me alone.'

And my mother literally ran away from me. She was wearing a long brown sheepskin coat and long colourful skirt. Her fashion sense hadn't changed. Her heart seemed to be the problem.

'Babes, I'm so sorry,' Curtis said. Back in the car, I just wanted him to hold me. I couldn't stop crying. Then I pulled away. 'Drive me home.'

Suddenly, I couldn't cope with his sympathy or his kindness. If I was on my own, then I had to be on my own. After that, I went into a downward spiral and put Curtis through hell. He tried to talk me through it and draw me out of it. But every time he tried to help me, I pushed him away. I expected him to understand exactly what I was feeling, even though I refused to tell him anything and wasn't even sure what was going on myself. Him being locked up meant we didn't exactly have much time to sort things out. And instead of letting him in, I pushed him out completely, in the same way that my mum had pushed me out. Our relationship took a long pause after that.

And then, in November, I saw my mother again. I was filling in a glamour lull by doing a promotions job at Gizmondo, a big electrical store on Regent Street. They had a new games console to sell and I was one of a crowd of girls handing out fliers and trying to persuade punters to come in for a closer look. It was just another day, just another job – until the moment I saw my mum walk by. In all the years since I'd moved out, we had never once bumped into each other by accident. Now, in a city of seven or eight million people, she was twenty feet away from me. Everything went very quiet and very slow. Should I stop her? Could I? The moment I asked the questions I knew that the answers had to be yes. I felt absolutely certain that she wouldn't reject me again. She must have had time to realise how awful it was last time. She was my mum, for God's sake. She must want to see her daughter.

I grabbed my colleague's arm. 'I need to speak to that woman,' I said, pointing to my mum.

'What do you mean?' But I'd already gone.

I caught up with Mum at a pedestrian crossing just up towards Liberty's department store near Oxford Circus. I put my hand on her shoulder to attract her attention; it was the first time I had touched her in ten years.

'Mum, it's me,' I said, full of hope.

'Oh, for goodness' sake, I'm getting sick of this!' she shouted. It was so loud and so awful.

'But, Mum . . .'

'You have to leave me alone. Stop following me. You have to stop.'

'Mum, I'm . . .'

'I said just leave me alone.'

'Is everything OK?' Oh, God. Suddenly people in the street were getting involved. The guy who spoke out was clearly taking Mum's side, having decided I was some kind of monster who was hassling her. A girl nearby was sniggering with her friend, loving the drama of it, getting ready for some sort of a catfight.

I realised this was one battle I could never win. I put my hands up in the air. This was it. 'OK, OK.' That was all I could think of to say. 'You don't ever need to see me again.' Then I turned my back and walked away.

My mum had turned me away in the street, in front of all these strangers. I couldn't even guess what was going on in her mind.

I walked away and finished my shift. Then I rushed home to shower and change. I was on total autopilot, in denial, as usual, about everything that was going wrong in my life. If I didn't admit it, then it hadn't happened, right? That night, I had a promo booking way over in Hendon. I had to big up a group of drinkers at a new Irish bar. And although I didn't know it yet, I was about to meet Mike Tyson.

CHAPTER NINETEEN

—————————————●—————————————

MEETING MICHAEL

People are always asking me about Mike Tyson. Everyone seems to have an opinion about him and about our relationship, and sometimes it feels as if everyone has spoken about it apart from me. So here it is: the true story of how I met Michael.

I was a zombie all the way out to Hendon for the promotions night. The agency had told me to be as glamorous as possible. It was a high-gloss, evening-dress event and all the girls would be looking amazing. That wasn't how I felt. I'd stood in front of the mirror at home looking at my face, tear-stained and exhausted after the incident with my mum that afternoon. I couldn't stay that way, so I'd wiped the tears away and painted on more make-up than ever. I'd chosen a long black dress with a deep slit down the front and diamanté straps that would glitter in the lights. When I got to the venue, I forced myself to smile. It was time to do my job.

The bar had just reopened after a major refit and it was full of tough-looking guys and hot-looking women. Along with the other five promo girls, I tottered around, flirting, laughing and getting the party going. 'You seen him yet?' one of the girls asked me when the doorman mentioned Mike Tyson. I'd only just been told he was going to be the guest of honour. I expected he'd stay in the VIP area. At that point, all I really wanted to do was go home and curl up on the sofa with my cat, Princess.

That was when I saw him. He was coming down a flight of stairs right in front of me. He looked great, really smart, in a slick white shirt and dark trousers. He had that walk that former sportsmen have – like their muscles are just seconds away from their old strength. He was sucking a lollipop. That gave me my first real smile of the night. Our eyes met just as the smile hit my face and he didn't seem to mind. It's a bit girlie and embarrassing to say so, but it really was like something out of a film. I felt as if everything was in slow motion. I liked how bright his eyes were, and how dark. For the first time that evening, I could no longer hear my mum's voice shouting 'leave me alone' in my mind.

And then he was gone. He'd been surrounded by a gaggle of people: the bar's owners, his bodyguards (like he'd need them) and some others. I was on my way back to the bar to carry on mingling when someone from his entourage called out to me. 'Did you hear what Mr Tyson said?' he asked.

'To me?'

'Yes. He wants to know if you'd like to join him for dinner later.'

'I'd love to,' I said, without really thinking about it. I didn't imagine that this was a date. It felt like part of the job. Then Mike himself came back. God, he was big. 'Bring a friend if you want, but just make sure you sit next to me,' he said. Then he smiled and disappeared. The invitation helped me get through the rest of the evening. My mum might have rejected me, but someone clearly thought I was worth getting to know. I was still numb from what had happened earlier, but my spirits began to lift a little as the night wore on.

It wasn't a particularly glamorous first date. We just went across the corridor to the restaurant attached to the bar. But I was about to walk into a different world. I took one of the other promo girls with me and I sat on Mike's left.

'It's Michael,' was pretty much the first thing he said, as he shook my hand. Then the questions began. I'd thought that, as a big-shot star, he might only want to talk about himself. Instead he wanted to know all about me. He asked about my life, my past, my family. I tried to skate over most of it – a midnight dinner didn't seem the right time for the whole story. But then Michael asked what I wanted to do with my life and it was good to put that into words. I said I wanted to design dresses, I wanted to work in fashion, I wanted to buy a bigger flat and live a better life. 'You'll be on TV,' he said when he could get a word in edgeways. 'That's what I think is going to happen to you first. You're going to be a TV star.' I laughed. It didn't seem likely, but it was nice to hear him say it. My confidence was so low at that moment, and, without even knowing it, Michael was building me back up.

Then he got ready to move. 'You feel like a club? You want to come out?' he asked.

'Yes, I want to go out,' said my friend, who'd been leaning in so close from my side all night that I'd thought she might fall face first into my dinner.

'I didn't mean you,' Michael said.

So I left the bar with him and got into his car. With us were two beautiful women plus a couple of Michael's friends. We were in a huge people carrier and as we piled in we got a lot of looks from everyone in the street. Then we got going. Our driver liked speed – or maybe he thought Michael did – so we were in central London fast. Everyone piled out at the Hilton Hotel on Park Lane, as Michael had decided we should hang out there rather than go to a club. And you know what? It felt natural to click across that marble floor in my heels with Mike Tyson at my side. I'd say I felt like Julia Roberts walking into the fancy hotel with Richard Gere in *Pretty Woman* if it wasn't for the implication. I suppose that was probably what some people who saw us were thinking.

Upstairs, on what felt like the 100th floor, Michael had an incredible set of rooms, all of which had vast windows looking out over the road to the blackness of Hyde Park. Everyone just hung out. There was no bad behaviour, no loud music and no noise. That suited me, really, because I was still feeling so raw over my mum. I wasn't up for a wild night.

Gradually, the others began to drift away and I was alone with Michael. But it didn't feel as if I was with 'Iron Mike' or 'The Baddest Man on the Planet'. I was just with Michael and he was a perfect gentleman. I'd felt an instant connection with him back at dinner. It kept getting stronger because we kept on talking. Michael still wanted to know all about my life, and I found myself telling him more about my childhood, my mum and what had happened that afternoon. He listened to me when anyone else might have turned away. It's funny, but I think he saved me by talking me through my issues. I'd felt so worthless that afternoon. I'd been close to a breakdown. But I'd done that promotions job, I'd met this man that the whole world was in awe of and he was listening to me. He took the time to build me back up. It's mental, but it was as if he'd been sent to me that night. We shared stories for hours, and I got to understand all the things that had made him who he was, just as he saw what had made me. I'm so glad I stayed.

When morning came, Mike had work to do. I quite liked that in him. He was in the UK as part of a big promotional tour, appearing in sports clubs and bars, talking at dinners and spending an awful lot of time in the back of his stretch limo. Apart from rushing home for a change of clothes, I spent the whole of that next day at his side. I sat with him in business meetings and listened as he was interviewed for a radio show. That night, we repeated the Hendon experience at another London club. I suppose it might have felt strange being with Michael as his guest rather than working alongside the other promo girls. In fact, it just felt normal. I was totally comfortable and stayed that way for the whole night.

The following morning, Michael got up even earlier. 'I've got to go up north. When I'm back, I'll call,' he told me, sipping camomile tea – his regular morning drink. I put a brave face on as I left the hotel. I knew that he wouldn't call. This was how famous people said goodbye. I headed home feeling deflated but not exactly surprised. I liked this man. He'd got me through a terrible few days. I liked that he never stopped asking questions and never ran out of things to say. I liked that he was so totally different from how I'd expected him to be. I'd thought famous people were self-obsessed and up themselves. Michael was the exact opposite. He was totally open to other people. What a shame I would never see him again!

I got the call about ten that night. It was from one of his assistants. 'Aisleyne, he really misses you. He's on stage here in Birmingham now and he really wants you here,' the guy said. So I jumped in a cab and was there in a couple of hours.

The next day, we headed back to London. 'I've never seen him like this with a girl before,' one of his people told me while I was waiting for Michael to come out of a meeting with the sponsors of the tour. It was such a nice thing to hear, but I couldn't help but wonder if the guy was bullshitting me. My self-confidence was still low and it all seemed a bit too good to be true. That evening, we went out for dinner in the West End and later that night, when we headed to Kabaret Club, I thought my worst fears were about to be confirmed. The club was packed, just jammed, with hot girls. That's it, I thought. I'm done for. When Michael left me at our VIP seats to talk to some guys at the bar I knew he'd not come back. Before I knew it, though, he was by my side. 'What's up, baby? I don't want you looking so sad.' And then he kissed me, full-on, in front of anyone who was looking (which was just about everyone in the club). The kiss was great, but having that mental connection was better. Michael said he'd been able to tell, without even looking, that I was unhappy when he was at the bar, so he'd come straight back. It was through crazy little things like this that he made me feel special – a feeling I'd wanted all my life.

That night, Michael did it again. We were back at the Hilton and Johnny O, one of his guys, turned up with a whole group of girls. They were gorgeous women, some of whom I knew from the London circuit. One of them sashayed right over to Michael and kissed him full on the lips. She danced in front of him and all the other girls were proper showing off too, trying to impress him. I've got to admit I was a lot more prone to jealousy back then than I am now, so I was royally pissed off! Johnny's a good friend now, but that night I wanted to castrate him. I was saved, though. Michael sent everyone away; he chose me over them. The thing was, it felt right. I didn't feel privileged; that was the way it was supposed to be.

No surprise that the papers were getting wind that something was up. One of Michael's security staff showed me a newspaper feature based on a big question: who's the blonde out with Mike Tyson? I read it all trying to see if anyone would be able to identify me. I wanted to stay a mystery. I wasn't with Curtis any more, but I was still worried it might hurt his feelings if he thought I had moved on already. I was also worried that if the papers tried to big up a story of a great romance, it might destroy things. I liked being in my bubble with Michael. It was private and normal and right. I didn't want anyone spoiling it.

The day after the article came out, Michael had to leave London again for some more promotional events. He asked me to come with him. It was just the two of us in the back of the limo as we headed towards Manchester. I was wrapped up in those huge arms and it felt so safe and so good. We still had so much to talk about. We'd both had crappy, unsettled childhoods. We'd both lost our way and hung out with what most people would call 'the wrong crowd'. He had converted to Islam and he knew a huge amount about different religions. We talked about all the faiths I'd lived through, about all the new rules by which he lived his life. 'You know what they say about me, right?' he said at one point. 'I'm different to that, OK?' But I'd already discovered that; he didn't have to tell me.

Things kept getting better. After Manchester, we went to the Midlands. During the first of the events there, I sat in the wings while Michael went up on stage to say his piece. But afterwards his assistant said Michael hadn't liked me being out of sight, so at the next event he had them put an extra chair on the stage, and I sat up there with my man. God only knows who the punters thought I was! At least the organisers didn't care. They just wanted their big man to be happy. He was. It was written all over that strong face. Were we getting too close too fast? I didn't know or care. In the back of my mind, I knew he was only in the country for a while, that he would be flying home to America soon. I decided to live in the moment for once. I'd worry about the future another time.

At the next big event, Michael was talking to the promoter while I did a hasty repair job on my hair and make-up. Frank Bruno was speaking at the dinner as well and came up to me backstage.

'Have you got any of that I can use?' he asked.

'It's lipgloss,' I said.

'That's OK.' He put some on. 'Got any mascara?' he asked, and we both started to laugh. We chatted for a while then he held out a big warm hand and gave me a lovely little bow. He was a gentleman. 'I'm going to say goodbye and leave you now,' he said. 'I can't be seen trying to steal Michael's girl.' I loved that!

Meanwhile, Michael was totally intense. Each night, he kept on talking, hour after hour, even though we both knew he'd be knackered the next day. Our minds seemed to fit just as well as our bodies. Once I'd started telling him about my life, I couldn't stop either. I told him all the things I never usually discussed with people unless I'd known them for years. I realised that for so long fear had closed me up. It was wonderful to feel able to be open. I knew he wouldn't judge me about my dad, about how I'd walked out on my mum, about how I'd lived in the hostels. He gave me a precious gift: confidence. I tried to give him love in return. It was clear to me that we had both been damaged by life. I was nowhere near the bottom of all his histories, but I was sure that given time I could repair some of his hurt. He'd already built up my confidence so much, and I hoped I'd be able to do the same for him if he needed it.

When we got back to London, Michael told me, 'Honey, you should go buy yourself some leather gloves today.' He gave me some money for those. It was another *Pretty Woman* moment, but it wasn't sleazy – he just thought long gloves looked classy.

That first week we spent together, I found out pretty quickly that as far as the media was concerned, Mike Tyson could do no right. Michael didn't drink, not a drop. One night, however, we were out in a big group and everyone was talking about a guy who had recently died. 'Drink a toast to your dead friend,' someone kept insisting, passing a bottle of champagne over to Michael. I could see that he had no intention of touching it, but everyone insisted, so he lifted it to his lips and that was it. But that was the moment when someone got a picture. The bottle had been shaken up a bit and it was foaming out over Michael's face, which made it look like he was glugging it. In the papers the next day, there was all this nonsense as if he'd been on a drunken rampage – 100 per cent false.

Then there was a story about a fight we were supposed to have been involved in but never even saw. 'Bloodshed At Tyson's Party', wrote one paper. Others had similar headlines. But we'd seen nothing.

When I asked the promoters the next day, they said the trouble hadn't begun till two hours after we'd left the club. We hadn't even been in the same city when the fight started, but still reporters were trying to pin bad stuff on Michael. He was used to all this crap. I, on the other hand, was outraged.

Meanwhile, Mike had a few struggles with life in Britain. 'What is it with English food?' he said one day towards the end of his trip. We were in a restaurant by the Thames. The waiter looked so bloody scared of Michael I thought he was going to keel over, and Michael didn't like his meal. 'I'll have a word,' I said. In my highest heels, I tottered over to the maître d' and made my point. The moment Michael's food had arrived, I'd known he would hate it. He'd wanted spaghetti and beef, but the restaurant had served something not unlike what Jessie had made back at the hostel with her frozen burgers. It really did look as if it had been thrown together. They sorted it in a second, though. We laughed about it as we headed down in the lift and on to Michael's next meeting.

'You know, the waiter nearly had a heart attack,' I said.

'Well, he nearly gave me indigestion.'

There were two more days left till Michael was due to fly home. I decided to enjoy every minute. We stayed together 24/7. I sat in on Michael's interviews and meetings and learned to read his moods. I could tell when he liked people and when he wanted to wrap things up. It was magical. For once in my life, I swear, I wasn't in denial. The Michael I saw wasn't the Mike Tyson that the papers wrote about. As far as I was concerned, that was a fictional character the press had created; to me, he was as gentle and sweet as Bambi, big eyes and all. What I think I saw was that Michael was the hunted just as much as the hunter. He was always surrounded by so many people, all fighting for his attention.

Saying goodbye was terrible. Michael asked me to follow him, and I felt sure that I would one day, but I had to stay at home and sort my life out. I'd known from the start that there was an end date when Michael would get on that plane and fly home. It was like a holiday romance, I suppose. But it had meant so much. Michael and I didn't make each other any promises. We didn't decide to try and live out some long-distance love affair. All we could do was wait and see what the future might bring. The good thing was that I knew that I'd made a friend for life. He had got me through so much. He had been there for me at a terrible time. We have a special bond and we love each other to this day.

I was devastated when Michael left, and couldn't be on my own. I called Tissam and went to stay with her for two nights while I got ready to face the world again. I left her flat determined to start afresh. I would bury the pain of my mum's rejection and make something of my life. Meanwhile, the London auditions for that year's *Big Brother* were less than a week away. Talk about destiny!

CHAPTER TWENTY

───────────●───────────

HELLO, *BIG BROTHER*

I'd watched *Big Brother* pretty much from the start. Why are some people scared to admit to enjoying it? It's always full of intrigue, drama and comedy, and summer just wouldn't be the same without that madhouse. What would we all gossip about if it wasn't for all those crazy people? I'd thought about auditioning for the show in 2005. That was when we had Anthony and Craig – bestest BB love affair of all time. It was the year we had Derek Laud, who I met and adored when we appeared together on another TV show. It was also the year of Kinga – ooh, the bottle! How could you, girl? – and of Makosi and her big mouth. I'd have loved to have shaken up that crowd. Maybe a lot of people who watch the show would be terrified about actually auditioning for it, let alone spending weeks on national TV, but that didn't worry me at all. I was a promo girl and a glamour model. Auditions didn't scare me. I wasn't bothered by the cameras either. I didn't think I had anything to lose by applying and I thought the whole thing would be a blast. I was gutted that I'd been too busy sorting my life out to apply the year before. So should I give it a go in 2006?

Becky made the decision for me. 'I will if you will,' she said. But then we got our dates mixed up and went out drinking the night before the auditions when we should really have been at home getting some beauty sleep and choosing our clothes. The next morning, Becky rang in a panic. 'The auditions are today, Ash, not tomorrow. I feel fucked. And I've got nothing to wear.'

'Well, I feel like shit too. We can't do it.'

There was a long silence on the phone.

'Can we?' I asked. It was so bloody tempting.

'Can we get there?' asked Becky.

'Do you think Zay would drive us?'

We decided that if we could get a lift from Becky's flatmate Zay, we would go for it. Zay said he would take us, and so the panic began. Still drunk from the night before, I pulled on a pair of jeans, a tight white T-shirt and thigh-high Dior boots. I worked on my hair, did my face and headed out.

We got to the end of the line 20 minutes before they closed it. Then the queue gradually snaked around. We waited in holding pens for two hours before being divided up into groups of ten and told to stand in front of a guy and a girl from the production company. We had to sort of say who we were and why we were special. I can't remember what I said. It was pretty nerve-racking, and I think I was probably really boring and just said who I was and what I did for a living. When I'd done it, a different producer wandered over. 'If I stamp your hand, you're going through to the next round,' he said. For some reason, I was feeling pretty confident, and my hand lifted itself up automatically as he walked past, just to make it easier for him. He ignored it, but then he suddenly came back. I was through. One of the security guards winked at me. 'I knew they'd want you,' he said, which felt good even though it was probably a lie.

The next part is where you say your little thing in front of a video camera. They ask you to describe yourself and say how you think other people see you. Some woman in the Ladies had just said she thought I was a 'ghetto princess'. I thought that sounded pretty good, so when it came to recording the video, that was how I presented myself. Looking back, I wonder if the woman might have been a member of the production team. Of course, it could just have been a spontaneous compliment, but maybe they suggested that label on purpose, knowing that if I rose to it, I'd somehow feel I had to live up to it. If the show is totally edited and controlled, then I suppose it's possible that they'd already decided what role they wanted me to play. 'I am like a princess, but, at the same time, if you cross me, I will fuck you up,' I told the cameras. That seemed like the kind of thing a ghetto princess would come out with. I said all sorts of pretty arrogant-sounding things and finished up by saying with a shrug, 'If you like it, you like it; if you don't, you don't.' Towards the end of our time in the house, Big Brother played our audition tapes to us, and I was mortified by mine. Thankfully, Pete told me that he thought it gave completely the wrong impression of me, which was reassuring!

After I'd recorded my video, I sat around while everyone else had their turn. We'd all been given a number and the producer said that if it got called out, we were through again. My number came up. Over the next few weeks, we began a series of secret meetings where you needed to remember a password to get into the buildings. It was cool as anything. I'd had a brief tomboy phase as a girl and had loved playing James Bond games. Now I felt like a spy for real.

I didn't try to be over the top at any of my sessions. It was much easier just to be myself. I admit, though, that my look might have gone a bit wrong sometimes. For my second big session, I wore a huge army jacket, three bras (to make my boobs look bigger), a cap and pretty much all the make-up I owned. I saw myself in a mirror at one point and I looked like a tranny with an attitude problem.

Sometimes during those interviews, it felt like everyone was picking on me. It seemed to me that the women on the panels were particularly tough. 'Who do you think you are? Do you think you're the next Chantelle [the winner of *Celebrity Big Brother* that January] or something?' they asked me. In hindsight, I'm sure they were deliberately provoking us all to see how we handled pressure. I think I've always been fine when I'm under attack, so I probably passed that test. It was funny, though; it wasn't just the people on the panels who tried to get a rise out of you. Other people in the groups were disruptive, disrespectful and rude. Was that just them showing off? Did they think that was the way to get ahead? Or could they have been plants from the production company? I never found out the answers.

'Right,' we were told at one session, 'what we need now is for everyone to fill out these forms.' They were vast, the size of phone books. I was flicking through the pages, convinced it was a scam. No one would read through all that, would they? Wasn't it maybe just a test as well? Maybe they didn't want to know what we wrote but how we behaved while we wrote it. So I just went for a little walk, chatted to a few people and did my own thing. I probably drove everyone mad, especially after I'd been to the drinks machine and got a fit of the burps. It must have been OK, though, because once again I was asked back for the next round.

That was pretty much when the jokes stopped. I finally realised that this was serious. I was close and I wanted it. Sure, it was 'only' reality TV, but I loved reality TV and if I was chosen, I would consider myself bloody lucky. Michael might watch from America. He'd see that he'd been right about me becoming a TV star, and, while we weren't officially an item at that point, I was glad he'd know I wasn't seeing anyone else if I was locked up in a house for three months. More than anything, though, I wondered whether my mum might be watching. Maybe, just maybe, she would see I wasn't so bad. Maybe she would want me back.

So I got really serious as the final few interview sessions approached. I also got insecure. They'll like her more, I thought. He's so much funnier. She's prettier. He's better dressed and looks much cooler. The anxiety and the doubts were out of control. What saved me was the fact that you don't know what they're looking for, so it's no use trying to be something you're not. They might have seen something in you that you don't even know about yourself. They're clever.

The worst bit was that we were sworn to secrecy. They say that if you tell anyone about it, you're out. So if you do the audition with a friend, you might just lose them. Becky and I were told we couldn't tell each other how far we were getting. Like scared kids, we complied, but we then broke the rules, both telling a mutual friend, Tammy. She had to perform a balancing act, knowing about each of us but pretending to the other she knew nothing.

The other big secret *Big Brother* people keep is that most housemates have spent time in a dummy house before the show itself. It's a testing session that takes place months before the series starts. You pack your bag, move in, meet your housemates, do tasks and evict each other. It's all taped and the producers are obviously watching as part of the selection process. I both loved and hated my time there in March 2006. I was with a group of really loud people, all massively acting up for the cameras. I felt overshadowed. I went to bed early on the first of my three nights in there, and they all voted to evict me! I'd been told that the people who do well in the dummy house often get selected for the following year's show. But even though I'd been booted out by my housemates, I was still hoping I might make it in that year. Some people probably get put off by their time in the dummy house. It makes it all very real and you get a taste of how paranoid you can become when you're in the house. I was different. I loved being locked away from the real world! I hadn't liked the other people and I was disappointed that I'd not made any friends, but if I hadn't truly had the *Big Brother* bug before, I did after the trial run. Surely the producers would see I could make good TV?

A month or so went by and I didn't hear a thing. I was gutted, but I carried on. Then it all changed. I was having a pedicure to get ready for a glamour job when my mobile rang. It was one of the series producers telling me I'd got one stage further for that year's show. I screamed and jumped out of the chair so fast the woman cut my foot. Freaky but true: the wound ended up looking just like the *Big Brother* eye. That has to be a sign, I thought. I'm going to make it.

Once again, though, I got knocked back. I didn't make it into the final group. I still had my *Big Brother* scar a week or so later when that year's show began without me. Like millions of other people, I watched Davina do her thing as Pete, Nikki, Grace, Sezer, Imogen, Mikey, Shahbaz and all the others walked into the house. What a bunch of nuttahs, I thought. They all looked mental. I totally dismissed them and said I was so glad I wasn't with them. I didn't mean it, of course. I was jealous. I'd got so close and now they were all in the house instead of me. I was gutted.

I booked a last-minute holiday to Turkey with Becky and Tammy to take my mind off the rejection. If I needed to plan another fresh start, I might as well do it in the sunshine. One day, we went on a cruise round the islands. There was a big sun deck and I had my top off so I could catch some rays when I realised that some guy had started taking pictures of me. 'Hey, what are you doing?' I shouted. 'You fucking pervert! You've got to delete those pictures, OK?' He didn't. I only found this out months later. After I'd made it onto the show, he sold the pictures to *The Sun* and spun some story about us skinny-dipping together in the moonlight. Full marks for forward planning, resourcefulness and fiction writing, but whoever you are, you should be ashamed of yourself.

Back at our hotel, Becky and I bitched away about *Big Brother*. 'They were all a bunch of circus freaks. I hated all of them. I'm glad I didn't get in,' I lied. Then my mobile went off. The producers were springing surprises. They needed me back in London fast, because I was going to be a housemate after all. I have never, ever been so excited, so happy or so petrified. It was absolutely brilliant.

But could it be true? For a few awful moments, I wondered if it could be some sort of scam. Was someone just trying to take the piss out of me? But it was real. A chaperone, a lovely man called Dan, met me in the arrivals hall at Gatwick. It was just after 5 a.m. Becky, Tammy and I had downed a bottle of champagne on the flight, and I couldn't tell if I felt so strange because I was drunk, exhausted or terrified. I suppose it was a combination of the three. 'Aisleyne, we need to take you home so you can pack a case,' Dan told me. 'You're going to need to take clothes you can wear again and again. But don't take too much branded stuff, because we'll need to cover up the logos. There's a list of other things you'll need here and information on toiletries and medications. Then we're going to a hotel for a couple of days.' Dan was talking to me as if I was a little girl, but then that was how I was acting. I kept letting out little screams. Could this really, really be happening?

I was pretty much in solitary confinement at the hotel. Dan had to take the TV and phone out of my room. He also took away my mobile. 'We're really sorry about all this. Sorry you can't even tell your family where you are,' Dan said kindly.

'Well, none of them knew where I was anyway,' I said. How crap to have to admit that I could leave the country and absolutely no one would miss me.

Then I started mouthing off about other things. If I asked Dan one question in those two days, I asked a hundred. Am I definitely going in? What should I wear? Who is still in? Who has left? Who did Dan like? Who did he hate? What was going to happen next? I don't think I got a single straight answer. They keep you totally in the dark, probably so that you're even more spaced out when you get in front of the cameras. But Dan did at least try to help when I begged to get my hair and nails done. 'We can't go far. Maybe we can find a place near here,' he said, before taking me out on a little prison break. The trouble was, 'near here' was deepest Hertfordshire. I don't think any of the hairdressers we found had ever had a customer under 50. Bless them, they did the best they could and it gave me some much-needed confidence.

I loved the way they got me into the house – even though it was terrifying. The producers told me a little bit about what was going on, but, as ever, they left me largely in the dark. They said the housemates were doing some kind of quiz. They'd have big boxes to open as prizes if they got the questions right. Some boxes contained toilet paper, food and things like that – and one of them would have me in it! I was thrilled. Ever since I was tiny, I'd dreamt of jumping out of a cake at a surprise party. Now I could jump out of a box on national TV.

I had a blindfold put on and I was led through the house and into the garden. They put me in my box and told me to stay quiet. Then they shut it all up around me. My heart was beating so fast and so loud I thought the whole world would hear it. This is it, I thought. This is real. I'm going into the unknown, in front of millions. Somehow, over the noise of my heartbeat, I could hear someone whistling. It was Glyn, although, of course, I didn't know that then. It was a weird feeling, knowing someone was standing a few feet away with no idea you were there. It made it all even spookier and scarier. What a way to join the show! What a rush!

Breaking out of that box and seeing the house was like dreaming. It was madness: a whirl of noise, colour, total excitement. I'd not even realised that someone else was in another box alongside me – Sam, who I'd actually met in the dummy house earlier in the year. We joined the other housemates together in a big crazy rush. I'd never been so up or so happy, and there was so much to take in. I was so caught up in it, I didn't think about the cameras once. I didn't have time. I had so many people to meet.

As in any situation, the lasting friends you make on *Big Brother* aren't necessarily the ones you're attracted to at first; they're the ones you gravitate towards over time. In my first few days, I was dazzled by the girls and just blown away by everyone. Pete was great – I loved his intensity and creativity from the start. He really reminded me of my mum and, because I remembered the woman with Tourette's who'd gone to Kingdom Hall with us years ago, I had more of an idea of what his outbursts were all about than some of the others. I thought Imogen was so beautiful. I thought Grace was obnoxious and loud, but I liked the way she dressed. I loved Nikki one minute and changed my mind the next. My feelings were all up and down, constantly changing – just the way the producers want them to be.

Sezer was someone who seemed to want to intimidate me from the first moment I arrived. It felt as if he thought it was his house. It seemed he wanted to push us all mentally, to keep us off balance and unhappy. 'The ones we don't like, we get rid of,' he said to me early on. I was amazed. You're trying to threaten *me*? I was thinking. Like I would be scared of him. 'Are you a bully, then?' I think I asked him. I knew I could stand up to him, although, as he got evicted a few days later, I didn't have to put up with his bad attitude for long. In the meantime, I enjoyed reminding him he was short. I wanted to knock him down to the size he was, not the size he thought he was.

Looking back, I've got so many good and bad memories from the house. All the mind games and bad mouthing were terrible. It knocks you down when people are great to your face then you find out they've said bad things behind your back. But there was so much fun as well. I loved going under the bed covers to try and talk boyfriends with Imogen. She had been dating the model Tyson Beckford and I wanted to tell her about my Tyson. I thought it was funny that they had the same name. I didn't want to announce it to the whole world, though, so I tried to spell it out to her in a game of hangman when we had chalk and a blackboard in the house. I don't think I really got it across! Imogen and I still see each other now and I also see Michael, one of the new housemates who came in from the House Next Door. And Pete, of course. I like having him as a friend.

I threw myself into everything. I could even cope with the 'State of Susie' task, when we all had to pledge allegiance to Susie, yet another new housemate. But the tension was always, always there, bubbling up close to the surface. I couldn't hide my feelings the night Grace got evicted. I'd been aware of the plotting and the whispers. Some of the younger girls had been bullying, intimidating and dissing Susie all week. They were picking on her because she was different, and I really disliked that behaviour. I thought Susie was a really nice woman – to me, she was a mother figure who genuinely cared about the rest of us – but even if you don't like someone, you don't do what Grace did. Which, in case you don't remember it or haven't seen it on YouTube, was to hug and kiss her friends and then pick up a glass of water and fling it in Susie's face.

The water must have hit her like a real blow. It was so quick, so violent, so nasty. I was outraged. It took all my willpower not to give Grace a slap. I kept asking her why she'd done it. Most of the other girls were carrying on as if nothing had happened. I wish in a way that I had done more to get back at Grace, but if I had I would probably have been thrown out. I'm glad I didn't lamp her. The row that it caused went on and on. I had a face-off with Lisa (the sweary Mancunian) and Mikey (Grace's boyfriend) in the bedroom that night, trying to get them to acknowledge how wrong it had been. Always fighting battles, I was. To this day, I still get the shivers when I think about what Grace did.

My series was a good one, though, don't you think? The House Next Door was brilliant in the end – terrifying at the time. I was up for eviction and Davina called out my name. I bought the whole story that I'd been evicted. I was terrified of facing the world and Big Brother knew I was having a breakdown, so I thought they were being nice to me. I thought I was leaving through a different room so I could get out of the house without being lynched by the angry crowd. The house makes you so paranoid. It plays on all your fears and insecurities. I don't really know why, but I was convinced that people must really, really hate me. But at least I'd get to escape them by making a quick exit out the back way, right? Then I found out the truth. I wasn't being evicted after all: I'd been voted into the House Next Door. It was unbelievable, and it changed everything. The moment I worked out what had happened, I began to get a new lease of life. Bit by bit, I got my self-belief back. I thought somebody, somewhere, must like me. I was so grateful that my adventure wasn't over.

But thanks, Big Brother, you still made life tough. I suddenly realised I was getting a new set of housemates. New people were flashing up on the screens as I moved into the House Next Door. I had no clue what it all meant. At first, I thought someone had messed up in the production team. It was as if they were playing audition tapes by mistake. But one by one, these people turned up in the flesh. I felt an immediate connection with Michael and tried to get to know all the others. It wasn't easy – and almost straight away I had to choose whether to evict Jonathan or Spiral. It was the worst. It was gut-wrenching. They were my favourites. I asked Big Brother if I could leave the show rather than choose, but I couldn't. So why did I pick Spiral? Because of my mum. I dreamt she might be watching. I thought if I supported the Irish by keeping him in, she might love me again.

And what about Nikki? She was 24 years old but as self-obsessed as a kid. I could have lied and pretended I was interested in all her dramas, but I'll never be a hypocrite. I quickly became bored of it and hiding that would have been dishonest. When I was up for eviction and in a bad place, I couldn't deal with any more 'me, me, me' from her. I was feeling ostracised, and I knew she'd nominated me. Then something else hit me. If I was being booted out that week, I had to speak my mind now. I'd be a hypocrite and a coward if I didn't. Out in the garden, I'd had my fill of Nikki. 'Boring,' I said as she went on and on. She stormed off, and someone said she'd called me a bitch. 'Know yourself, little girl,' I told her. That line came from the heart. The biggest lesson I've ever learned is to know who you are and to stay true to it. It's about being honest inside, about facing up to your life and your limits and everything else. I love that people get what it meant and still repeat it to me even now. I started a trend with that phrase – how good is that?

I was gobsmacked when Nikki was evicted, especially as we were all up for the vote and I'd been sure I'd get the chop. I thought Nikki was favourite. I was sure everyone at home would love her girlie dramas, even if I didn't. Poor Pete. I knew he needed help when he was on his own and I tried to talk him through it. Everyone talks about the triangle with me, Nikki and Pete – her fancying him, him sort of fancying her, me sort of fancying him, and on and on. When she was sent back into the house in the second-last week, it was a headfuck. She kept making little digs and saucy comments against me. It was a war. She was undermining me, chipping away at my confidence, making out the world hated me. It was hard to take. The more she said, the more paranoid and depressed I got. I thought everyone hated me outside. I got terrified about ever facing the world again. It's easy to play with someone's mind in the house. What was worse was that Nikki won over most of the others. We were all desperate for clues from her about what the public thought of us. She just kept making out that I was the bad girl and that I'd drag other people down. Richard must have believed her. I felt him turn against me from that moment on. Big Brother kept calling her in and telling her off, but she wore me down, I'll admit it. Only Imogen stayed true to me, but she was evicted later that week. I had to live without her friendship and support as well. It was horrible.

The whole thing is so much tougher psychologically and more draining than you would imagine. Everything affects you; everything plays with your emotions. I found myself dealing with every emotion through food: If I was sad, I'd eat; if I was happy, I'd eat; if I was bored, I'd eat. So what do you do when you've failed a task, lost most of your shopping budget and the food isn't there? The amount of hours you're allowed to sleep has an effect on your mental state, too. No matter how late we'd stayed up the night before, we'd have to wake up early the next morning and that can make you ratty all day, and more likely to be snappy. We had one clock, on the cooker, and if that stopped, my goodness, did that freak us out! Even the temperature the rooms were kept at was controlled by Big Brother, and that could affect our moods, too.

It's such a pressurised environment. I used to watch the programme and get driven mad by how often everyone burst into tears. 'Why are these freaks crying all the time? They can't have had much going on in their lives if they cry over stupid stuff like that!' I'd scream at the telly. Then, of course, I went on and cried all the bloody time. My excuse is that everything is heightened in there, and even small stuff really matters to you because you have so much time to think and overanalyse things. There are no distractions – no music, TV, books or magazines, nothing to take your mind off yourself.

In the end, though, I think it did me a lot of good. That chance to reflect turned out to be just what I needed. A couple of years after the show I sat alongside Vanessa Feltz, Germaine Greer, Derek Laud and a couple of others on *The Culture Show*. How amazing is that in itself? Anyway, we were talking about George Orwell's *1984*, which I had to speed-read for the show, and the idea of a surveillance society.

'I hated being in the house. It was incarceration, just awful,' said Vanessa, who had done *Celebrity Big Brother* a few years earlier.

'But that's probably because of where you'd been beforehand,' I said. 'I loved it. I begged the *Big Brother* producers to let me stay for ever. For me, it was a cocoon. No worries over paying bills or where to live. No violence, no bad influences. I thought it was like a refuge.' And I did. Funny that the *Big Brother* madhouse gave me stability when the hostels screwed me up so that I kept on repeating the same old mistakes for far too long.

The prison task was a high point, really good. I can't believe I was first to see it all – the tunnel to the secret world was under my bed. Us prisoners had to act as if we were having a terrible time and keep quiet about the room of luxury at the end of the tunnel. It sounds a bit complicated now, but at the time it was a real laugh!

On the other hand, the argument I had with Spiral was a low, really bad. It began over something so trivial – we were talking about food, I think. It got pretty ugly. He said I thought I was special, but I didn't and I never have. That fight affected me so much. Sometimes it's not just a game show, it's real life. But I look back now and think that dealing with Spiral and his comments helped me make the journey. With hindsight, maybe I should have cared a bit less, but at the time it mattered and I couldn't hold back. It's strange, because Spiral and I look back on it and think it's funny how stressed we got.

When we completed that task, our reward was letters from home. I lost it. More than anything, I wanted mine to be a letter from my mum. She had to be watching me. She had to know I was there. So this had to be her moment to say something. Hardly a day had gone by without me thinking of her brushing me away on Regent Street. Every bit of me wanted the note to be her saying we could start again. But it wasn't from her. It was a few lines from my dad. That was OK. I wanted to hear from him, so that was good. But if I'm honest, the real reason I cried was because I'd wanted my mum to say she loved me. What a mess I was that day.

All the time, I still worried about what people outside thought about me. I know I can come across as if I've got an attitude, and I was always totally convinced I was public enemy number one. 'That girl thinks she's black, why does she talk that way?' I was convinced that was what people would be saying. 'Why is she so prickly? What's she trying to prove?' The truth is, I wasn't trying to prove anything. Some people accused me of being fake, but I was trying to shed my old skin, not pull on a new one. I wanted to shake off all the attitudes and the layers of protection I'd needed in the outside world. That was why, in the end, the house made me strong.

I proved it when Grace returned. She was allowed back into the house for 21 minutes on her 21st birthday. I wanted to smack her so much. I always want to smack bullies. *Big Brother* knew that, too. They knew how passionate I got. But I reminded myself that it's no good sinking to the bully's level. Also, it was her 21st. I remembered mine. It's a big moment. I didn't want her to be looking back when she was 40 and remembering that on her 21st birthday she got a slap from me on national TV. So I handled it. I said my piece, but I held back and didn't do anything physical. Poor Pete, too scared of confrontation to come out of the loo and face her.

Funnily enough, Grace and I are OK with each other now. Well, we tolerate each other. I saw her and Mikey at a party a year or so ago and she tried to wind me up.

'That's a very demure dress. That's not like you,' she said.

'I might be demure, but I still don't have any knickers on,' I said.

It was a joke, right. But I liked seeing Mikey's eyes light up and Grace's fake smile disappear. Funnier still, all this time later Nikki and I are cool. I don't think anyone watching would have predicted that.

At long last, on 18 August 2006, we came to the end of the road. I was in the final. How had that happened then? I tried to calm myself down by putting my energy into worrying about what to wear. It didn't really help. I showed Richard and Nikki the outfit I wanted to wear and they laughed. A wave of insecurity hit me, so I dressed down. That day, I was thrilled, excited, terrified. Part of me wanted to get back out there into the world. Part of me was too scared. A lot of me just wanted to stay in the house. However crazy it was, I felt safe there, safer than I did anywhere else. But I had to get ready for the final night. I'd been trying to save booze all week and I'd not eaten all day so it would kick in fast. I thought I'd need to be drunk for when they threw things at me outside. I couldn't believe that, after all those weeks and all those evictions, I was still there. It all got too much for me. I had a total panic attack in the afternoon. I dropped to the floor in the bedroom. The producers must have been worried. 'Will someone get Aisleyne to the Diary Room!' boomed the voice over the PA, sounding scared, when I started to hyperventilate. I had pins and needles running up my whole body, from my feet and legs up through my chest to my lips.

'Breathe into the bag, Aisleyne,' said Big Brother. 'Sit down and calm down and breathe.'

'Can I just leave through the back door?' I asked when I was able.

The voice was kind but firm. 'Aisleyne, get back into the house and get ready for the final evictions,' he said when it was obvious I was OK. Oh, God.

It was as if the world had been turned upside down on that last night. I watched the others get evicted one after another. I was saying goodbye to them – when I'd thought they'd all be saying goodbye to me. I was gobsmacked by that, but not as gobsmacked as them! Time shot by until we got right to the end. Then there I was on the sofa with just Glyn and Pete left. All the pretty girls had gone. I was up there with the nice guys, the housemates I liked and respected the most. How the hell had it turned out like this? I was flattered and overwhelmed and finding it hard to breathe, let alone think.

Then Davina spoke to us again: 'You are live on Channel 4. Please do not swear.' She announced my name as the next evictee. I have to admit that, yes, I was a bit disappointed. A tiny part of me had dared to think I might go further. After all, I'd been expecting to hear my name all night and I hadn't. But all good things come to an end, right? I was ready for the next part of the game. I went up that stairway to the double doors. Then I walked into the unknown. When you get through those doors, it's the real deal, the most surreal and scary thing ever. Why had I decided to wear heels, I wondered as I started to descend the massive steel staircase.

'We love you, Aisleyne!' That was the first cheer I heard, from a group of girls way away from me, as I tottered down the steps towards Davina. They must be people I know, I thought. Who else would shout that? The next shock was seeing how pregnant Davina was. What a great woman. Go, girl! Everything else just crowded in on me, all the banners, the shouting, the noise. It's funny, that moment I left the house was the first moment I thought, I'm in *Big Brother*. That was the first time it felt properly real. You're on your own a bit in the madness. I wasn't sure where to go or when. I just looked up, soaked it in and tried to get to Davina. I did my best promo-girl poses for the photographers. The flashes and the jostling are intense, and I couldn't believe how many pictures they were taking.

That first live interview was a total blur. You really don't get any help. You have a few moments while the adverts are on to catch your breath and try and check your hair, then you're on, with no clue what Davina will talk about, what anyone thinks of you or who you might spot in the audience if you take a sneaky sideways glance. I saw my dad, suddenly, and that took my breath away. My dad's here for me, I thought, and that meant a lot. Seeing the other housemates all lined up was emotional too. Michael pulled up his shirt to show a T-shirt with 'Go Ash!' written on it. It was strange watching myself in my 'best bits' video: someone who had a real chip on her shoulder who finally, fortunately, softened. 'Aisleyne, you've been on the biggest journey of anyone in the house this year,' Davina said. It felt like it that night. It felt like I'd run a fucking marathon.

My chaperone, Dan, was the first person to hug me when the live interview was over. It was great to see him. 'You know you were worried about getting promotions work?' he whispered in my ear. 'Well, you won't need to do that job now.' He told me that in the final calculations, when it had been just me, Glyn and Pete up for the public ballot, I got 22 per cent of the votes, which was pretty good. Then he led me into my first press conference. And they say the *Big Brother* house itself is mad! This was pandemonium. Everyone was laughing, shouting my name and yelling out questions. 'But I haven't even won!' I kept saying. I had five minutes with the show's psychiatrist after that. But how anyone would have known if I was unbalanced, I don't know: the whole world was clearly off its head.

As if it wasn't mad enough, I then met Russell Brand! I was thrown right into *Big Brother's Big Mouth*. My first thought when I saw Russell was how the hell did he get those jeans on? They were so tight! My second thought was that I wanted him to flirt a bit with me. I liked the twinkle in his eye. He was so quick and he had so much energy on that show. He swept us all along on a wave of hysteria. The big shock was how much the audience knew about the show. Wow! They'd really been paying attention! They knew everything. They hadn't missed a moment. One of Russell's other guests nearly made me cry – with happiness. It was Paul Morley, the journalist and all-round cultural pundit. Russell asked him what his highlights of the series had been. 'Aisleyne: Aisleyne going back into the house, Aisleyne's laughs, Aisleyne standing up to all the cruelty she's had to put up with, Aisleyne becoming a feminist icon when she didn't even know it and no one else knew it in the house.' I was dumbstruck. All the time, I'd been so terrified that people thought badly of me. Then someone like Paul said that. What a night! And it kept getting more surreal. When Russell's show ended I moved on to my second press conference. It might sound silly, but I couldn't believe the reporters all knew my name. It was late and the conference went on and on, but I was loving every minute.

Tissam and my friend Portia screeched and hugged me when I got out of the press room. All the housemates were allowed two friends or next of kin to join us in the hotel they lay on for your first night out. Before we left the studios, though, I had to see my dad. It must have been nearly 2 a.m. when we spoke. The lights were low and he was still wearing the darkest of sunglasses. Back on the drugs, then, I thought. Nice one, Dad. 'I'm so proud of you, princess,' he said, hugging me tightly. I felt proud and happy, too.

I didn't eat or sleep in the hotel that night. But I did look at some of the press cuttings that the *Big Brother* people had handed me. I'd had my picture in the papers a few times before, but nothing like this. There was page after page, paper after paper. One of them had this article where the amazing TV critic Grace Dent said I was 'the most alpha male in the house', and that included Sezer. I wasn't sure how to take that at first. Now I'm proud of it. Some of the stories shocked me – I couldn't believe the guy from my holiday who'd said I'd gone skinny dipping with him! Some of the stories people had sold about me didn't surprise me. They weren't that shocking, and, as far as I was concerned, they reflected worse on the people selling them than on me. The only thing I'll say to anyone else going on *Big Brother* is watch out for the pictures your mates take of you when you're drunk. They'll end up in the press one day. Mine did, and some of them were pictures I'd far rather have forgotten!

At the crack of dawn on my first day of freedom, I was driven off to meet a panel of agents. There were nine of them, a mix of men and women, all intense and desperate to be wanted. 'We've got a BMW outside for you if you sign with us,' yelled one. 'Sign with him and your career will be dead before lunchtime,' said another. 'Aisleyne, we've got Channel 4 ready to give you your own show.' 'We can double what anyone else gets you out of the papers.'

I was trying to act cool when my mobile went. It was Curtis. 'Excuse me, but I've got to take this call,' I told them all.

'Hello, Miss Superstar,' he said.

'Curtis, I'm in the middle of a meeting. Are you cool with everything?' I couldn't remember how much I might have said about him (or indeed anything else) when I was in the house. After a while, you really do sort of forget about the cameras and just mouth off as normal. Had I maybe hurt Curtis in some way? Had I caused any problems for him in prison? Everything was OK, thank God.

'If anyone deserves good things from all of this, then it's you,' he said. 'You just go for it.'

So I was back facing all the agents. After getting dazzled by the sales pitches, I went for the agent Imogen had picked. They got me the usual eviction exclusive, with the *Sunday Mirror*, and it turned out I needed the cash. I was driven back to my flat in King's Cross to get a change of clothes and I found I was in rent arrears. My new life wasn't all quite as glamorous as I'd thought.

Glyn and I joined forces for our first big photo shoot, in a massive, gorgeous suite at No. 5 Cavendish Square. It is the swankiest, loveliest place. Even if you do nothing else after *Big Brother*, you do get to hang out in some amazing places with no big bill to pick up at the end. Although Glyn very nearly didn't: he fainted just after we arrived and bashed his head on the window frame. Thankfully, the *Mirror* had laid on the absolute best hair and make-up people. Oh boy, did I need them. I looked a state. I'm glad they were the kind of people who enjoyed a challenge. They were also far nicer than I'd expected. I thought the reporter would want all the sleaziest stories. I thought that if I didn't give them anything, then he or she would make something up anyway. But it didn't work out that way. They seemed to want to talk about the real me, and that felt good.

The whole thing was a blast. The *Mirror* had put me in the Hilton in Angel for the weekend. The 24-hour room service was the best – not that I could eat much, although Tissam helped make up for that. They had a car waiting to take me back to Angel from Cavendish Square. They wanted me wrapped up in towels and a gorgeous fluffy bathrobe so the paps couldn't get any pictures of me and spoil their exclusive. One of the photographers had a dig. He was a big, fat white guy that I'd seen outside plenty of clubs in the past. He looked mean and he was. 'All right, Aisleyne, enjoying your 15 minutes of fame? Oops, that's one more minute gone,' he said as he fired away at the cab windows. Charming.

Signing deals is like winning the lottery – how else can you get that much money that fast? After the *Mirror* I had an offer from *Nuts*. They wanted an interview and photos, and they paid the most they had ever paid for any *Big Brother* girl. I was proud of that. But it was all a bit like being in a crazy jungle without a map, let alone sat nav. Most of the time, I didn't know what I was doing or where I was going. Apparently, I was always saying thank you for everything. Thank you for taking my picture. Thank you for speaking to me. Thank you for wanting to see me. I got hoarse saying it on the busiest days, but they were such brilliant fun. Moving up a level from the old glamour shoots was an eye-opener too. My guy in his bedroom in east London had done a good job, but going to real studios with all their staff and equipment was a rush. The freebies were even better. When the style people on one shoot said I didn't have to pay for the £800 hair extensions they'd just done, I nearly kissed them!

Working with male models was mental as well. I did one shoot for *more!* magazine that had me as the power woman with four men crouched in front of me on dog leads. One of the guys – and they were all fit as anything – was a bloke who lived near me in King's Cross. It was bizarre: I'd seen him loads of times out at clubs and now he was my pet dog! When there were other models on the shoot it could make it all seem a little less lonely. I did feel a bit isolated at first on some of these big magazine shoots, when everyone else seemed to know each other and I was on my own in front of the cameras.

Who else did I get to meet? Dermot O'Leary, of course, who is just as pumped up and handsome as I'd expected. His wife's a lucky woman. Justin Lee Collins and Alan Carr on *The Friday Night Project* were brilliant too. And I just loved the banter with Chris Moyles when I was a guest on *Big Brother's Big Mouth*. It's all just a wall-to-wall whirl of people and performances. I loved it. If I regret anything, it's that I didn't motor ahead even faster and do even more. In those first wild days, someone apparently turned down a slot on *Richard & Judy* because they thought I needed to rest for a big photo shoot the next day. Rest? Versus Richard and Judy? 'I can bloody sleep when I'm dead,' I said when I found out. I still can't believe I never got to sit on their sofa – or at least not yet.

I did do plenty of other good things, though. One was the premiere of Adam Sandler's film *Click*. I was deafened by people screaming out my name. I went over to one bunch to sign autographs and then turned to head on into the cinema. I swear to God the person signing autographs right next to me was Adam himself. And it was my name the people kept shouting! 'Hey there, thank you for coming,' he said to me as I passed him by – as if he'd have even had a clue who I was.

With so much madness going on, you're bound to make some mistakes. I did. There was one lovely journalist who interviewed me for one of the weekly magazines. We did the chat, all of which was taped, then, when the recorder got turned off, we carried on chatting. She didn't say that the rest of the conversation was off the record and I didn't think to ask. I liked her and I thought she liked me. We had a coffee and gossiped – starting off with all the usual girlie stuff and then getting onto bad men and bad times. I thought I'd made a new friend that day.

Then the magazine came out. 'The Night I Nearly Died Losing my Baby – by *Big Brother*'s Aisleyne' was the headline. Every word of what I'd thought was our private gossip was in the story. I was mortified, but I guess at least I learned that journalists can be like taxi drivers. The meter is always running and they never give anyone a free ride.

Do I hate that so many people recognise me? Are you kidding? I love it. Sure, it's weird that complete strangers suddenly have opinions about you. But I'd signed up for it by going on *Big Brother*, so I'm not going to complain. I'd put myself up for public auction, so the least I could do was play the game. So what if I couldn't get public transport for a while? Top tip for anyone who does go on *Big Brother*: put some money aside, because you'll probably want to get cabs for quite a while afterwards.

You also need to be ready for people around you selling their stories. They're crap, but you have to believe they reflect more badly on the people selling them than they do on you. Most of them are sad and predictable. Dad had a bit of a dig at my mum in his story. He must have thought he was sticking up for me, but, I'm not going to lie, it hurt. I just pray he didn't use the cash to get high; I couldn't have that on my conscience. One thing that nearly stopped me going in the house in the first place was worry that somebody would expose my dad. That was why I was so shocked that he put himself in the firing line by selling a story with a photo of himself. But I later learned that my worst-kept secret had already been exposed, not by any dodgy people from Dad's past wanting to make a quick buck and not by anyone we knew, but by some old bird that Curtis had been seeing. She really went to town on us. She posted loads of stories on the Internet saying my dad was a junkie and dealer. It was wicked and bizarre. It wasn't as if she'd even met me, let alone my dad. She became my Internet stalker – not as scary as the couple of physical stalkers I've endured, but certainly the nastiest on the web. Anyway, once the words were out there, they just kept on popping up online. So Dad had a rough time. But gems shine through the dirt, and I got over it quickly enough. It actually helped in a mad way, as I didn't have to worry about keeping the secret any more.

My mum's family all had journalists camping out on their doorsteps for weeks. Notes promising them big money were put through their doors every day. Some of them could probably have done with some extra cash, but they never said a word. Someone else was silent. My mum. I'd secretly hoped she might be there in the studio or the crowd on eviction night. I'd remembered watching almost in tears as families had been reunited in other years. But it wasn't to be.

CHAPTER TWENTY-ONE

SLIPPING BACK

Maybe a year after leaving the house, I nearly threw it all away. I'd spent a big slice of the autumn of 2006 on the personal appearance circuit. It's the weirdest business. Some of the events are totally surreal. A lot of the time, I was just asked saucy questions based on some racy interview that had just been printed in *Nuts* or something. Other times, I had to judge guys doing sexy dances or stripping off in front of me. It's not bad work, girls! I pretty much loved all of it. I got to travel, meet new people and I got paid just for being there. Sure, I've been booed a couple of times – everyone who does these kinds of events has been. But you know what? The people who boo you still want your picture and your autograph at the end. Funny that.

The boys are the worst. One time, there were two who shouted out the whole 'Who are ya? Who are ya?' thing when I was on the stage. I felt like yelling, 'I'm the one who's picking up £3K for being here, who the hell are you?' But I just smiled and waved and gave it everything. What gave me the biggest buzz was that it was hardly ever the girls who tried to trash me at PAs. The only time any girls did, it all got turned around. I was in the loo and I could hear two girls talking. 'That Aisleyne from *Big Brother*'s here tonight. When she goes on stage, let's boo her,' one said.

'Hi, girls.' I came out of the cubicle with a big smile. We sorted it. We talked dresses. We got on great. Problem sorted.

I also got lucky with my new agent. I'd felt like a change, and I went for the company run by Darryn Lyons, the paparazzi guy with the pink mohican. They were brilliant at keeping the invites flowing and showing me how the other half live. The freebies and goodie bags at the posh parties got me the most. It's amazing that the richer people are the more free stuff they get. I also discovered the wonderful, well-paid world of photo shoots abroad. I'd head off to a beautiful beach or an exotic location overseas and spend several hectic days posing for photos which were then sold to newspapers and magazines. Despite what you might think, it was very hard work! Up at the crack of dawn, make-up on and head out early with the photographer to a suitable spot on a beach, cliff top, or wherever to shoot a set of photos. Then back into the hire car to another location, change into a fresh swimsuit in the back of the car or behind a rock, quick touch-up of the make-up and back in front of the camera for another set of pictures. This would go on all day, often without a break, until the light began to fade. At the end of each day, I was usually so tired that I just wanted to get back to my hotel room and crawl into bed – I never got to enjoy the nightlife. However, the rewards have been fantastic. My photos have sold globally and I get mail from fans worldwide. I still get a good income from even the earliest post-*Big Brother* pictures, and practically every time I glance through the lads' mags in the newsagent's there'll be a photo of me taken in some foreign hot spot in one of them.

In the summer of 2007, when I did one trip to New York with Imogen, I also got to meet someone very special to me: Pras Michel of the Fugees. I've always admired his work because his raps are really meaningful. They're not just about bitches and hos. The way we met was mental, but then my life usually is. Apparently, he'd been Googling his single 'Ghetto Supastar' and I kept popping up, partly because that was the song they'd played to accompany my 'best bits' on *Big Brother*. He read a bit, saw a few clips and then emailed me through my website.

I'm not going to lie, I was flattered. This Grammy-winning superstar wanted to get to know me. But we're all just human. 'How do I know it's you?' I wrote when I finally replied to the email. 'How do

I know it's you?' he emailed back! We bantered a bit for a few days and then we sent some ordinary, non-press photos to each other on our personal emails. We chatted online, spoke on the phone and then planned to meet up in New York. Pras came to our hotel to take me out to dinner. We got on brilliantly. He was earthy and real, just the way he'd been on the phone. He was wearing jeans and a brown-and-blue top, no bling, no attitude. His friends were just as cool and we all decided to hit the town after we'd eaten. The clubs weren't as good as the company. They were huge and a bit commercial compared to London. All the other girls were skeletal and scary looking. One got proper cheeky with me and seemed up for some sort of fight. I pulled an old trick out of the bag and told her to know herself. 'Hey, you don't play,' Pras told me as the girl tottered away.

We met up again the next day. He was working on the trailer for a documentary film he'd made and he showed it to me in a recording studio. He had spent ten days with the down-and-outs in the Bronx to raise awareness of homelessness and all the issues surrounding it. I remember thinking how much depth there was to him. He tipped me off about something else as well. 'See this man? He's going to be our next president,' he said, pointing to a picture on his website of him with Barack Obama. He was about to go to a fundraiser for him, and I wish I could have stayed to join him. As it was, Imogen and I flew home the next day. But I knew I'd made a real friend in Pras. It's great that we still see each other today.

Another good guy I met was Kanye West. I was on my way into Movida when this guy called me over. 'Is this place any good?' he asked. I said it was. 'Do you want to come in with us?' he asked. I said I was fine and I was on my way in already. 'Do you know who that is?' he asked, pointing over towards his group of people. It was like twenty questions! There were six or eight people in a little huddle and I didn't recognise anyone. Not even Kanye West. 'Come on, join us,' the guy said, so I did. When we got inside, I was finally introduced not just to Kanye but to his mum! She went everywhere with him – God rest her soul. They were both good people. Kanye was shorter than I'd imagined, the way a lot of famous people are. He was very chilled. He wasn't a womaniser and certainly wasn't picking out girls. He was just having a good time with old and new friends. We had a table and talked about music and clubs and everything. He was big on making sure everyone had a drink and there was a good vibe. He danced on his chair at one point and we all joined him. The next thing I knew, two girls threw their knickers at Kanye. In front of his mother! The whole thing was mental, but it turned out to be more about business than sex. Two lovely sisters had set up an underwear company and had thrown the pants at him to get publicity for the label. You've got to admire them for that. Funnily enough, a year later I became the face of the company for a while. Coincidence or what?!

The best thing about life post-*Big Brother* was that I'd managed to save up a decent deposit and get a mortgage to buy my King's Cross flat. That was something I could never have done without the show. Knowing I had that to fall back on changed everything. It was the security I'd always felt I needed. And I needed it more than ever, because, a long way from my new public life, one final storm was building up. Once again, it was my dad.

The nightmare had begun back at Christmas in 2006. We'd planned to play happy families at my aunt's house. What a joke that turned out to be. Dad was late picking me up and when we got to my aunt's he went straight to bed and didn't wake up for something like 14 hours. When he did surface – super-early on Christmas morning – he was clearly on something. We all did the denial thing, pretending everything was normal while we opened presents with the children. Then, when my auntie was in the kitchen making breakfast, I confronted him. Mum had taught me tough love. I had to tell him that he needed help. But I got nowhere. My auntie, bless her, then had her say. Nothing.

'I left my mobile in the car. I'm going to get it,' Dad said. He got in and just drove off. It was 9 a.m. on Christmas morning.

I nearly threw up next time I saw him in spring 2007. He had a hole in his leg, a wound as big as a football. His leg had swollen horribly. His foot was blue. His room smelt rotten, like someone had died. Nan and Grandad were there. I can't imagine how they must have felt seeing their son lying there with such a hideous drug-related infection.

The doctors said they might need to amputate his foot to try and save his leg, though in the end it didn't come to that. I wanted to scream at him, 'You lost me for years, you might lose your foot – what else will it take for you to stop?' But I'd seen in the hostel days that addicts only save themselves when they hit their lowest point. Dad had always been picked up just before he got to the bottom. One of us would always leap in to offer him a room or some kind of reprieve. Then it would all start again.

Back in my own flat, I couldn't stop shivering. All I could see was the infection seeping out of my dad's leg. All I could think of was my mum writing some angry letter to me that she would never send. I'd started to fear the waves of doubt that washed over my my family and other people I'd known in my life. There was depression, addiction – all that kind of thing had to be genetic, right? At first, I tried to conquer my fears by reading up on it. If I understood these illnesses, I felt, I would be able to tackle them. I also tried to take my mind off all the shit by having my flat decorated. I wanted the walls to be clean and gleaming white. I had friends round as often as possible so that there was always laughter and good karma in my home. I wrote to my mum, as I always did when I felt I needed some kind of new start. But she sent the letter back unopened with 'Return to Sender' written all over the front of it. I cried for hours over that. Not long after I stopped crying, I found out that Curtis had a child.

I got the news in the most bizarre circumstances – at the Mobo Awards in September 2007. I'd been to the ceremony the previous year and had been invited back. There was the usual long red carpet with lots of photographers. I sat in the VIP area and had a dance with my friend Keisha Buchanan of the Sugababes – the TV cameras caught us when another mate, Ne-Yo, was performing on stage. I was having a great time. Then, after the awards had finished and I was preparing to move on to the after-party, I spotted a friend of Curtis. I headed over to talk to him. Curtis and I hadn't been in touch much in all the time since *Big Brother*. He was still in prison, after all. I still cared for him so much, and, while I didn't think we could ever go back to where we were, once he got released I did want to find out how he was doing. His friend floored me with a single question. 'Have you seen Curtis's kid yet?' he asked. I gasped for air. I had no idea what he was talking about. A baby? Had Curtis had a quick shag on day release and not taken precautions? His friend told me the truth – and I'm not sure if it was much better. The child was ten. Yet Curtis had never once mentioned him to me. I've always said I can handle anything if it's the truth; what I can't handle are lies. And if Curtis had lied about this, then what other secrets might he have kept from me? I thought I knew everything about Curtis. Apart from Marc and Michael, he was the only one I'd ever told everything about myself. This felt like losing my mum and dad all over again.

I rushed to the loos in the middle of the party and broke down. I cried long and loud. So many lovely people tried to comfort me – most of them complete strangers who were just being kind. But nothing could pick me up. I can't remember getting home from those awards. My night had begun with me on top of the world. It ended with me lower than ever.

As I tried to deal with those feelings, more cracks started to appear in my façade. I hadn't yet worked out the divide between what I did for my career and what I did for fun. I wasn't a doctor, a banker, a nurse or a teacher who worked and then went home. I was 'Aisleyne', a 24/7 product I'd created by going on TV. So if I failed as Aisleyne the product, I'd fail at everything. I didn't know how to handle that possibility. And the low blows kept coming. One night, I got turned away from Movida. The club had decided to ban all *Big Brother* stars. I know I shouldn't have let it get to me, but it felt like a kick in the teeth just when I needed it least. It all started to drag me down.

I sat alone in my flat. I looked at my life. All I could see was pain, loss and isolation. Emptiness seemed to fill my room. I was drowning in it. I told myself that the world would be a better place without me. I told myself that my mum and dad wouldn't miss me. For far too long, I had expected too much from Curtis. I'd needed him to be more than just a partner, to replace my mum and dad. I know now that that's too much to ask of anyone. But that night in my room, I thought I had no one left who really loved me. I knew it was self-pity, but I didn't have the strength left to control it.

I did the weakest thing I've ever done. I took an overdose of painkillers. I was drifting in and out of consciousness when something quite incredible happened. My mobile lit up and rang. It was my friend Soldier, the same man who had come to the door and saved me when I'd had my first miscarriage a few years earlier. He had rescued me then; now he was doing the same again. If we do all have a guardian angel, then he truly is mine. He called for an ambulance, which took me to hospital, where I stayed for two days.

I am ashamed of that episode. It seems to me to be the ultimate in weakness, and I have always tried to be strong. I know it might be hard to understand. After all, I had been through much worse. The difference was that I had never felt so alone before. From the outside, my life at this point would have seemed just perfect to anyone looking in, and in a way that made me feel even more helpless.

I debated whether or not to admit to having attempted suicide, but I decided to do it so that anyone reading this who might have similar feelings can see that they are not alone. It's vital to get help if you feel hopeless or depressed, and the contact details for the Samaritans are at the back of this book. I wish I'd never done such a dangerous thing and I feel so lucky to be alive.

When I got back to my flat, I vowed that nothing would take me so low again. And if Soldier's voice had saved me from dying, my mum's voice told me how to stay living. I remembered the things she had told me about independence, respect and strength. In the good times, she had got all of that through her work. It was time I did the same.

CHAPTER TWENTY-TWO

―――――――――――●―――――――――――

MOVING ON

With my mum's voice telling me to be independent and strong, I decided to look after my own career again, just as I had done before *Big Brother*. So I set up my own management company, Aisleyne Limited, to run all my business affairs.

For me, one of the best things about running my own company is that I now own my pictures: no more model release forms that make everyone else rich. Today, if anyone wants to write some crazy story because they think I'm dating someone that I've never even met, then that's fine, because they'll need a good picture to illustrate it and I'll get a nice royalty when they use it.

Shortly after I decided to go it alone, I was approached by Unique Collections, a family-run clothing business based in Manchester. They'd noticed pictures in the press of me wearing their dresses at some red-carpet events. Then, one morning in September, they saw me on *This Morning*, presenting an award at the annual Prima High Street Fashion Awards. I was wearing a gorgeous, floor-length gold-and-black dress from their range. They picked up the phone and called me.

When we met, they said they'd like to sign me up as the face of their company. I thought that seemed a bit too short-term, and I wanted to be more involved. 'Look,' I said, 'my mum had her own fashion shop and she taught me to design pretty much before she taught me to read or write. I've studied fashion and I want to make clothes of my own. Can I work with you on the dresses themselves?' After a lot more talk, the family said yes. The new label was to be Unique by Aisleyne.

I focused on the kind of clothes I wanted to wear, the kind my friends would wear. I spent days up in Manchester drawing up a capsule range, I got the samples made, sorted the fabrics, then we sent it all out to be manufactured over in France. It was such hard work, but it was the best feeling ever. The first collection came out for spring/summer 2008 and it just felt brilliant to be using my skills. I loved being back in the mad, artistic world my mum had inhabited. That initial range was sold in around 30 or so boutiques around the country as well as online, and it was an immediate success.

After that, everything kept getting more exciting. I didn't get the bus to Brick Lane or head to Camden. I got to catch the Eurostar to Paris to meet other fashion designers there and work with the best. And as Pras was there doing some recordings, I also got to catch up with him. It's great when things work out.

Then, with my mum's wise words from the past still echoing in my head, I decided to strike a new deal. I took over the whole Unique by Aisleyne operation in time for the launch of my autumn/winter 2008 collection, which was launched at Pure London, a major fashion trade show. I'd expanded the range to include coats, trousers and a greater variety of tops. It was at Pure that I realised how far I'd come on my journey. There I was with my own stand in this huge exhibition at Olympia, with models and promotions girls who were there working for *me* and modelling *my* clothes.

Now that I own the company name – my name – I've got big dreams. I want to do more club clothes. I want to do really glamorous special-occasion stuff. I want to make some really cool men's T-shirts – the list goes on. The great thing is working with all the fabrics I loved as a girl. I mix a bit of my mum's wild style with the way I know girls live today. While the fashion business is tough, I get a thrill from the whole thing. I feel so lucky to be part of that world. I love making contacts and all the deals I get to do. I like charming my way into getting samples, finding out who has the capacity to make what I need and get it all noticed. It's really inspiring promoting something I feel so passionate about, too, and I've shown off the label in photo shoots for *Star*, *OK!*, *Love It* and all sorts of other magazines.

Creativity and design were in my mum's DNA. They must be in mine. I reckon that gives my clothes an edge and explains why I love everything about the business. I surprise my newsagent by buying *Drapers Record* along with *OK!* and all the other gossip titles. 'I'm a working girl,' I tell him. I just hope he knows what I mean! One of the things I hated about the hostel years was that no one there ever talked about what they did for a living or what their dreams were. I talk about it all the time now, because I'm so proud of it. I'm not embarrassed about wanting more.

Two things that are definitely not in my DNA are running – running anywhere – and camping. In 2007, I did both. The running came about after I mentioned Uncle Billy's brain tumour in a magazine interview. Another friend of mine was suffering from the same illness and it was all I thought about. The charity Brain Tumour UK got in touch. They wanted to know if I would help them raise their profile – and raise some cash. So that's why I started doing 10K runs (well, 2K runs and 8K walks, but I always swear I'll make it to the finish line even if it takes me two weeks). An even bigger thrill came when they asked me to be a patron. It was an act of trust. It meant I couldn't screw up in any other part of my life because I had a duty to represent them positively.

So what got me camping? Charlie Brooker. We met not long after *Big Brother* and he got me to come on *Screenwipe*, his programme about television. My first appearance was fabulous. He set up a mini-reality TV programme to show how misleading the editing can be, and I was one of the contestants. After that, I did loads of other cameos for him. I ended up becoming the show's mascot when we came up with the Chavleyne character, the (hopefully) exaggerated ghetto-princess version of me. Off set, we really hit it off, but our friendship had a tough test when we went to Glastonbury.

I got my tent in Argos. It cost £7.50. Charlie's tent was supplied by *The Guardian*. I think it cost more than most people's houses. All he had to do was throw it in the air and, hey, it was a tent. I swear it had wall-to-wall carpets and central heating. If mine looked pathetic when I finally worked out how to put it up, that was nothing to how it looked the following morning. It rained like hell that night. I cried myself awake, I was so wet and cold. My tent looked like a paddling pool. I think it probably was a paddling pool. I'm sure I could have claimed against Argos under the Trade Descriptions Act!

Charlie, in his luxury palace, wasn't happy either. Bless him, he will moan about anything. He reckoned that the druggies with the light sticks were targeting him over everyone else in the million-strong crowd. He reckoned they deliberately kept him awake. So that morning we agreed that our little experiment was over. We legged it to the cottage that *The Guardian* had rented a few villages down. It had hot water and proper beds.

When we were at the festival, I had an awakening: I totally fell for Dan le Sac vs Scroobius Pip, poetic rappers whose every word spoke right to me. And I made friends with the Marley Brothers. How cool is that? Stephen Marley had always been an idol of mine. I followed them from tent to tent at Glastonbury, then, when they were on tour later in the year, I got to go backstage and meet them. They're totally grounded guys; I met their sons and felt really connected to them. Poor Stephen is a bit of an agony uncle for me now. I ring him or Charlie up when I have some girlie crisis and need a man's viewpoint. Cockroaches in my flat? I phone Charlie. Need to know what to wear for a TV show? I'll pick up the phone and at least one of them will give me the answer.

It was funny that I met a very wild woman just as I discovered some very grounded men. She was a Saudi princess and she floated into my little crowd at The Edge club one night in Holborn. She was beautiful and free-spirited. She had a driver outside and when we left the club we headed back to her house by the river. It was mind-blowing. It had a vast kitchen and living area on the ground floor with the garages, then a huge sort of harem-style room on the first floor. It was all soft fabric drapes, a mega-sized version of the ones my mum had made all those years ago in Regent's Park – I always said she was ahead of her time. There was a bed or sofa-type thing the size of a tennis court, there were cushions everywhere and the whole place reeked of sensuality. There was a whole wall of mirrored shelves holding more alcohol than I've seen in any bar. Upstairs in her bedroom, the princess had a vast roll-top bath in the middle of the room. There was a huge TV that rose up out of the floor, a pair of vast dressing-rooms and, best of all, a perfume room. It was as big as my bedroom in King's Cross, with shelf after shelf of special-edition bottles of every perfume you have ever seen. The place was every girl's dream.

We kept in touch for a while. She'd ring me up when she had a crisis, but hers weren't about cockroaches. 'Darling, I've just spent £27,000 in Dolce & Gabbana. Do you think it was too much?' she asked me once.

'It depends what you bought,' I replied. 'Did you get the whole company?'

Today, I still see some of the best of the *Big Brother* people, by which I mainly mean Pete, Imogen and Michael. Pete's never stopped surprising me. 'We've got an outfit for you,' his girlfriend Cherry told me before one of our big nights out together. It was a little pant and jacket combination with a real '50s vibe – if they wore wet-look, wipe-clean black rubber in the '50s, that is. I got the feeling we were in for quite a night.

'So what kind of club is this?' I asked Pete.

'Wait and see. It's a total madhouse. You'll love it.'

We got a cab down to Brixton and Pete pointed out the club from the end of the road. It was an old converted church and when we got inside I nearly fell over. It was a full on sex club, a rubber club, a fetish club, a leather club – I suppose you could call it pretty much anything. But Pete's description of 'madhouse' didn't really do it justice.

We found a little sofa on the edge of a walkway near the toilets, where we sat and watched the goings-on. It was fabulous fun. I don't think I've ever seen so much flesh on display before. Baggy, saggy flesh, that is. Why do people leave it so late before they decide they want to go to these kinds of places? No wonder Pete and Cherry were so popular. The outfits kept getting better. There was leather, latex, rubber, plastic. All sorts of chains and piercings. Two women dressed as nuns with habits that gaped open just where you really don't want them to. A lot of fishnets on the men, uniforms on everyone, privates on parade. On the other side of the corridor, where there were lots of dark corners, there was also a lot of sex getting started.

'You've not been down to the dungeon yet,' Pete said suddenly. He had that huge smile on his face. I loved living with him in *Big Brother*.

Oh. My. God. There are loads of reasons why I can't describe what we saw down on that level. One of them is that I'm really still trying to process it. But here are just a few phrases to mix up if you want to paint a picture. Old man on his back. Totally naked. Woman in stilettos. Balls. Standing on his.

We all headed back upstairs fast. The little sofa was still free so we set up court again and sat back to watch the show. Quite a lot of people came over and talked to us. Within minutes, I was being chatted up by an old guy holding a roll of electrical wire. That was pretty much when I decided it was time to go. But thanks, Pete and Cherry. What a night!

So in the past year or so, I've learned to go out, have fun and relax, rather than worrying about everything too much. But one thing that does get to me is the speculation about footballers and me. Trust me, no matter what people might assume, I've never wanted to be a Wag. I don't think it would be that fulfilling. You can spend a lot of money and feel you're living a great life, but so what? It's not your money you're spending and you'll never be sure your man will be faithful. He's a hot footballer, after all, and other girls will throw themselves at him all the time. Life's enough of a headache without all that, I say. But I am glad I've met plenty of footballers and got to know some of them.

One of the first was Michael Essien. We met at a 2006/07 New Year's Eve party in the West End. I'd dressed up, of course. I was in a beautiful butterfly print dress and feeling good. I was with my friends Tammy and Charles, and halfway through the night Charles called me over. 'Meet my friend Michael,' he said. I didn't recognise him, but I liked what I saw. He was smart, in jeans with a shirt and waistcoat. We tried to talk, but it was so loud and so crazy we could hardly hear each other. He asked for my number so we could try and meet up and talk another time. I gave it, without really thinking about it. I got caught up in the New Year madness after that and never found out exactly who this Michael was. He called a few days later and asked if I wanted to go out and celebrate Chelsea's latest win.

'Are you a fan?' I asked.

'No, I play for them,' he said.

Oops! But he wasn't offended, and we went clubbing again. Didier Drogba was with us, and we went in and out through the side door of the club to avoid the press – as if that's really possible. It got in the papers and a while later when I was having a late-night Chinese meal in Soho a girl came right up to me. 'Are you sleeping with Michael Essien?' she asked, just like that. I nearly choked on my pak choy. 'Excuse me? How can you come up to my table and ask something like that?' I had my chopsticks in my hand and I was all ready for a kung fu battle. But she turned on her heel and disappeared. Her friend came over and apologised for her.

I liked that Michael was never on an ego trip. My hairdresser had been talking about that sort of thing when he'd been doing my hair for the New Year's Eve party. 'When stars are at the top of their careers, they are always in love with themselves,' he'd said. 'It's ego overdrive. They might be looking at you, but all they're seeing is themselves.' And people say hairdressers are airheads – that was one of the sharpest comments I've ever heard on the subject. Michael wasn't like that, though. He was always aware of everyone around him and when we went out in a big group he made sure we all felt comfortable all the time. But once we'd had a few dates, we realised that we didn't quite gel. We've stayed friends, though, and I'm glad about that.

Jermain Defoe was the next player I was linked with. He's someone I'd seen loads of times out and about. He's a nice guy, but I couldn't take things further. He's good friends with one of Curtis's friends and I thought I'd be rubbing Curtis's nose in it if we dated. Plus Jermain's ex-fiancée was an acquaintance of mine. We have a laugh, though. We go to restaurants and I've been to his house a few times, and we always text each other when we read another silly newspaper story saying we're a couple.

And Peter Crouch? I met him at a club, as well. It was someone's birthday party, I think. He and his mate were chatting to me for ages, but it was loud in there and Peter said he wanted to talk in a booth where it was quieter, so off we went. He's not my type, but he's funny and we had some fun banter – until his missus walked by. She got the wrong impression and got upset. 'Babe, I promise you, nothing is going on,' I said. But she wasn't hearing it and I decided it was a good time to leave! Their argument was getting nasty and was much reported by the press at the time. So, really, that's enough of footballers for me. Life's stressful enough without all that aggro.

But me and Mike Tyson? He's someone I'd never want to lose. He was back in Britain during summer 2008 on another promotional tour. I was filming *The Friday Night Project* the day he arrived, and I headed to see him as soon as the studio work was done. He was in a club ready to give a speech, surrounded by all these girls trying to get close to him. They all disappeared as soon as they saw me! We fell back into our old ways straight away. It was as if we hadn't seen each other for two weeks rather than two years. It was just a shame that visit was even shorter than the last one, but we made up for lost time and painted the town red.

On his last morning in the UK, we were drinking camomile tea as usual and talking away about me going to America. And that time I felt ready to visit him there. The last time, I'd not wanted to see him in the States because I didn't think I'd made enough of my life. In 2008, there was still a lot that I wanted to do, but I was going in the right direction. I loved that I would be able to pay my own way when I went to see him and felt proud of how far I'd come since that night in Hendon when we'd first met.

Even leaving aside my fashion range, I've had so many wonderful opportunities. I've been an agony aunt for *more!*, which was much harder work than I'd expected and quite emotional. Some of the stories in the letters stayed with me for a long time. I've also worked as a columnist for *Reveal*, writing about *Big Brother* series 8 and 9 in a weekly column. I've had various radio spots, including several stints co-presenting on Choice FM with the lovely Martin Jay. I've really enjoyed doing TV work, too. I've been followed by a TV crew for *Aisleyne*, my own fly-on-the-wall reality show. I've worked for all five of the terrestrial channels, doing all kinds of TV – talk shows, documentaries, drama series, you name it. But what gives me the biggest buzz is doing comedy. I just love it! Doing *Dead Set*, the *Big Brother*-set zombie series created by Charlie Brooker was amazing too – though spending five hours in make-up every day was not. I normally spend a long time trying to look glam for work. Who knew it would take even longer to look terrible! We had really early calls on the shoot because of all the time we spent in make-up, but the stylists were great company and Jaime Winstone was so cool and down to earth to work with as well. I loved that it was such a big production – an army of people behind the scenes pulling it together. I was so proud that Charlie had made it all happen. He'd talked to me about the idea a year and a half earlier, and now it was finally being filmed. My modelling work has become much more varied, as well – everything from fashion spreads for *OK!* to sets of smouldering poses for lads' mags or the red tops. So when people ask me if I regret doing *Big Brother*, what do you think my answer is?

What's even better about the way life has turned out is that I've made so many wonderful new friends. People say the entertainment industry is full of fake, shallow people, but that's not been my experience. (Well, not with most of them, anyway!) I still have Becky, Tammy and a few others from the old days, but I have now got a great bunch of new friends, too – some in the public eye, some not. Amy (I mean *the* Winehouse!) is one of the ones everyone seems most interested in. I don't get why people are so fascinated about how we met and what we've got in common. We actually met through a mutual friend, the one and only, the beautiful Katriona. She was always saying Amy wanted to meet me. Anyway, one evening I was doing a PA in a West End club and Katriona was there. Later that night, she got a call from Amy. I was making so much noise with Michael from *Big Brother* in the background that Amy couldn't hear what Katriona was saying. 'Who's that loud girl?' she asked. 'Ask her if she'll come over,' Amy said when Katriona said it was me. Naturally, I had to check my diary to see if I was free! Turned out I was, so over to Camden we went. The strap on my shoe broke as we headed over to Amy's house, and pretty much the first thing she did at whatever time it was in the morning was mend it! She got a needle and thread out and stitched it back together while we got to know each other. And when I left at dawn she gave me a pair of her ballet pumps to wear home. That's the Amy I know now, not the one the papers go on about.

She reminds me a lot of my mum. She's so beautiful, so talented and so creative. She's got a real motherly streak, too. She's a wild spirit, but she's practical. I just love the vibe in Amy's house whenever I go round. Her friends are so varied. You don't need the telly on there for entertainment. The conversations going on are always deep. That's a bit like going back to my childhood, as well. It reminds me of all the arty people who came round to my mum's and talked all night putting the world to rights.

People ask me daily how Amy is. I call her a lioness. She is so much stronger than everyone thinks. She can bounce back from anything life throws at her and I love her strength. So, just for the critics, what do we have in common? We're north London girls. We've both had boyfriends who were in jail. We do different jobs, but we have similar outlooks on life. She's a real girl, and real recognises real.

One thing about my new life that I still can't get over is how many emails I get to my website every day. No surprise that some are a bit dodgy. Why do so many men think I'll be interested in their bits? But most of the messages are lovely and lots make me cry. I get a lot from people who are bullied. Recently, I got one from someone I don't even know but who sponsored me on my last charity run. She wrote that she wants her daughter to turn out like me. That's someone else I can't let down now I've turned my life around.

So life is good. Life is great. The other day, a journalist asked me two questions. The first was where I wanted to be in five years' time. I struggled to come up with an answer. I've never had a five-year plan. Growing up in Mum's mad, creative house meant I never saw life as a set of stepping stones towards some great goal. I just try and get on with things and see what happens. In five years' time, I just know I'll be living a decent life and loving every minute.

The next question was what I'd learned in the past five years. That one was simple to answer. That denial is a bad thing. That none of us should close our eyes to what's going on around us. And that we can all turn our lives around and make them better. I can't bring myself to look at the tapes, but I know that in the *Big Brother* madhouse I kept on saying 'know yourself'. 'Believe in yourself' works just as well.

That's where I've got to today.

USEFUL CONTACTS

There is always someone who can help you if you look hard enough. Asking for help when you need it will make you stronger. Here are some contacts that may be of use to you or your friends.

Addaction
Drug and alcohol treatment charity
www.addaction.org.uk
67–69 Cowcross Street
London
EC1M 6PU
Tel: 020 7251 5860
Fax: 020 7251 5890

Alone in London
Working with young vulnerable people
www.als.org.uk
Unit 6
48 Provost Street
London
N1 7SU
Tel: 020 7278 4224
Email: enquiries@als.org.uk

Barnardo's
Leading children's charity
www.barnardos.org.uk
Tanners Lane
Barkingside
Ilford
Essex
IG6 1QG
Tel: 020 8550 8822
Fax: 020 8551 6870

Brain Tumour UK
Supports brain tumour patients and funds research
www.braintumouruk.org.uk
Tower House
Latimer Park
Chesham
HP5 1TU
Tel: 0845 4500 386
Email: enquiries@braintumouruk.org.uk

Bullying UK
Help and advice for victims of bullying
www.bullying.co.uk
Email: help@bullying.co.uk

Connexions Direct
Information and advice for young people
www.connexions-direct.com
Tel: 080 800 13 2 19
Text: 07766 4 13 2 19
Advisors available 8 a.m. to 2 a.m.

Kidscape
Working to keep children safe from bullying or abuse
www.kidscape.org.uk
2 Grosvenor Gardens
London
SW1W 0DH
Helpline: 08451 205 204
Tel: 020 7730 3300
Fax: 020 7730 7081

The Miscarriage Association
Offering support and understanding
www.miscarriageassociation.org.uk
c/o Clayton Hospital
Northgate
Wakefield
West Yorkshire
WF1 3JS
Tel: 01924 200 799 (Monday to Friday 9 a.m. to 4 p.m.)
Fax: 01924 298 834
Email: info@miscarriageassociation.org.uk

The Prince's Trust
Helps young people move into work, education or training
www.princes-trust.org.uk
18 Park Square East
London
NW1 4LH
Tel: 020 7543 1234
Fax: 020 7543 1200
Email: webinfops@princes-trust.org.uk

St Mungo's
Offers homeless people in London access to housing and hostels
www.mungos.org
Griffin House
161 Hammersmith Road
London
W6 8BS
Tel: 020 8762 5500
Email: info@mungos.org

The Samaritans
24-hour confidential emotional support
www.samaritans.org
Chris
PO Box 9090
Stirling
FK8 2SA
Tel: 08457 90 90 90
Email: jo@samaritans.org

24-Hour National Domestic Violence Helpline
Run in partnership between Women's Aid and Refuge
Tel: 0808 2000 247
www.womensaid.org.uk and www.refuge.org.uk
Email: helpline@womensaid.org.uk or info@refuge.org.uk